On Being a Jew

On Being a Jew

James Kugel

The Johns Hopkins University Press
Baltimore and London

Originally published in 1990 by HarperSanFrancisco, a division of
HarperCollins Publishers
Johns Hopkins Paperbacks edition, 1998
9 8 7 6 5 4 3 2 1

The Johns Hopkins University Press
2715 North Charles Street
Baltimore, Maryland 21218-4363
The Johns Hopkins Press Ltd., London

Library of Congress Cataloging-in-Publication Data

Kugel, James L.
    On being a Jew / James Kugel.
        p.   cm.
    Originally published: New York, N.Y. : HarperSanFrancisco, c1990.
    ISBN 0-8018-5943-3 (pbk.)
    1. Orthodox Judaism—Miscellanea.   I. Title.
    [BM582.K85   1998]
    296—dc21
                                                            97-44004
                                                            CIP

A catalog record for this book is available from the British Library.

For R.

Contents

Foreword

Following is a record of certain conversations that took place between the young man, Judd Lewis, and the banker, Albert Abbadi. Abbadi, a friend of Lewis's father, is the managing director of a small private bank in midtown Manhattan; the conversations all took place in his office.

PART I

On Marrying a Protestant

AA: Come in, come in, my friend. You don't need to tell me why you asked to see me. I'm very glad to hear it! Poetry is certainly a wonderful thing—you know I'll take little convincing on that score—but, alas, in our day at least, it will hardly pay the rent. Was it your father's gentle urgings or your own experience as a miserable graduate student? Little matter. In any case, the offer still stands—in fact, I have taken the liberty of contacting Mr. Michaan of our international office —

JL: No sir, I'm afraid you don't understand. I haven't come looking for a job. I guess it's true that the life of a graduate student is miserable, but that's not news, and the reason for my visit is. I came to tell you that I'm getting married.

AA: Well, that *is* good news. Permit me to sit down—you sit too. You know, I'm younger than your father; still, things like this make one feel like an old man. Married. I wasn't too much older than you are now when I first met your father, and you . . . were probably two years old. Well, we will have to *arroser ça,* as they say. Have you ever drunk Araq? It's very common in the East—and the right thing for such an announcement. Here, give it a taste. It's best to drink it without water.

JL: Tastes like Pastis.

AA: Hm, yes. Well, tell me, who is the young lady?

JL: A woman I know in Boston. I know you'll like her. I hope you'll meet her before the wedding—in fact, that's one of the things I came

3

to speak about. I wondered if you might be able to recommend a rabbi to perform the ceremony. You know my family isn't particularly religious; we're not members of a temple. I think you're the only religious Jewish friend my father has. I was hoping you might be able to put me in touch with someone, someone you know personally.

AA: Well, I certainly could do that. But isn't there a Jewish chaplain at the university? They do this sort of thing all the time. Believe me, they don't mind if you don't go to synagogue every week! Why don't you make an appointment to see the chaplain? He's much more likely to be able to fit in with you than any of the people I could recommend.

JL: I already have seen him. But he said there might be complications. That's why I came to you.

AA: Oh. I see. Well, I suppose I should have guessed. In other words, the young lady is not Jewish.

JL: No.

AA: Is she interested in converting?

JL: She's Presbyterian. Her family's not religious either, so my being Jewish is not an issue. But she says she doesn't see any reason why she should give up her family tradition in order to marry me, especially since neither of us is particularly interested in religion.

AA: And you say?

JL: I agree with her. Pressuring her to convert to my religion wouldn't make any sense. I guess that used to happen a generation ago, when it was assumed that the wife would just follow her husband in all things. But that isn't how it works nowadays—at least I certainly hope not in our marriage.

AA: I see. Well, it seems that you have made your choice.

JL: But I still do want a rabbi for the Jewish part of the service. Her minister in Philadelphia is going to do the Christian part, but we wanted a rabbi there, especially for the glass-breaking ceremony. The

4

rabbi I talked to at the university is Reform, but he said that he himself didn't do mixed marriages. In fact, he said there were very few rabbis who do.

AA: I see. He didn't by any chance explain to you why such rabbis are so hard to find? You see, the marriage ceremony in itself is very straightforward—in fact, there is very little of a ceremonial nature that is even required in order for a Jew to get married. But weddings still are of great significance. While it is theoretically possible for someone like yourself to marry a non-Jewish girl and remain committed to Judaism—perhaps even become more involved in Judaism as a result—it is, at least statistically, not very likely. What is more, any children born of a Jewish father and non-Jewish mother are considered by Jewish law to be non-Jews. So instead of being a wedding, such an occasion is, from the standpoint of Judaism, more like a funeral. Pardon me if I am overly dramatic. That is why rabbis are reluctant to participate in such a ceremony.

JL: Don't you know someone who might do it? Because—I hope you won't take offense—this is something that has always struck me, long before it became a personal issue, as narrow-minded and, frankly, a little stupid in Judaism. Certainly religion is mostly a matter of a person's beliefs. If that's what makes me Jewish, why should my status suddenly change just because the woman I'm marrying happens to believe something a little different from me? Or believes nothing at all? For that matter, why is a Jewish spouse who's an atheist somehow better for a Jew than a Christian spouse who's an atheist—not to speak of a Christian spouse who actually believes in basically the same God as we do and tries to lead the same sort of religious life? This obsession with bloodlines and "marrying Jewish" has always seemed to me like some primitive holdover—as if Judaism were less a religion than some great tribe with its own marriage taboos.

AA: Well, of course, you're right, Judaism is in this regard rather different from most of the world's great religions. If you will permit a banker a commercial analogy, I might say that while the various creeds of this globe have by and large organized themselves into large and impersonal joint-stock corporations, in which all may become participants through a relatively simple transaction, Judaism has remained essentially a family-owned affair. As such, the conduct of its "business" is not merely a matter of certain assets and liabilities being shared by a constantly changing population of stockholder—or, to leave off the analogy, it is not simply a matter of the "beliefs" you mentioned being subscribed to by an amorphous infinity of believers. Rather, Judaism might be described as the way of understanding proper to one large family of people, whose own bloodlines connect them as much as their beliefs and which, therefore, are considered by all to be very important. To be a Jew is, in large measure, to belong to this great, sprawling family. And, like any family, this one takes a lively (and none too respectful) interest in its younger generation's marriage plans, not the least because the family's whole future ultimately depends upon them. Now you cannot see why your standing as a Jew—which, to be frank, is for you in any case a relatively minor concern

JL: That's not entirely true. I may not be, by your standards, a religious Jew, but what you've just been saying implies that that is only part of the picture. I've always considered myself Jewish, and I've never made any secret of that fact, even though my name is not particularly Jewish-sounding. In fact, people usually assume I'm not Jewish. But I suppose the same thing must happen to you too.

AA: In America, yes. To someone brought up in this country my last name seems to identify me only as foreign, indeed, if anything, Moslem. But as for your name, to the informed observer it is also transparently Jewish. "Judd," in your generation of Jews, is a popular stand-in for the Hebrew "Yehuda"—no doubt the name of some departed grandfather or uncle for whom you were named. As for "Lewis," a generation or two ago it must have been "Levine" or "Levinsky," a casualty to Americanization, just as these names themselves were Slavified versions of the original, gentilic "ha-Levi," an honorific title your ancestors appended to their names to indicate their descent from the tribe of Levi in biblical times. So (not to put too fine a point on it) your "Yehuda ha-Levi" is obvious to any who care to look into things.

JL: My father must have told you.

AA: No matter. Let's return to the point. You have made no secret of being a Jew, I believe you on that, and it is certainly to your credit. But in the present circumstance it is largely irrelevant. Allow me to speak bluntly, like the Jewish uncle that I am to you. You want a rabbi
• to take part in your wedding to this young lady. Even if such a rabbi could be found, I am baffled as to why you should want him there. As I mentioned, the ceremony itself is of little weight in Judaism. It is only the larger question, "To Jew or not to Jew," that has any significance, and on this you have spoken clearly. You will marry a Protestant. Perhaps you will still go through life regarding yourself as a Jew, but for me and your other fellow Jews you will have taken the one step which, if not utterly irremediable, by and large always leads to a dead end. A Jew who is irreligious or utterly ignorant of Judaism but nevertheless marries another Jew will at least pass on something—his share in the family business, as it were. But a Jew who, by marriage, gives up his descendants' share, passes on nothing, a memory; and the choice itself is a judgment on his own Jewish standing, even if, by law, he remains a Jew to his dying day.

JL: But that's the part I don't get. How do you know my children won't be Jewish? I certainly plan to bring them up with a sense that they're Jews and all that that means. If they're not considered by Judaism to be Jews because their mother is a Christian—well, they can certainly convert when they grow up if that's what they want. And if they don't, then maybe their children will—in fact, they themselves may end up marrying Jews. The important thing, it seems to me, is that my children know where they came from. I'm certainly committed to giving them that, and if that means my learning more about Judaism, well, frankly, I'm not against that either. I'd like to teach my children about Judaism, about where they came from, and bring them to Sunday school or Hebrew school every week. But what I can't understand is why now, at this crucial juncture, when I am about to get married and determine the whole course of my married life and how my children are going to be raised, Judaism says to me, If she's not Jewish we don't want to know you exist.

7

AA: That's a fair question, to be sure. In fact logically you may have a point. But I believe the greater weight of argument to be on the other side. There is something ultimately correct in the angry act of rejection that you attribute to Judaism by its refusal to sanctify your marriage. Because beyond all the good resolutions that you may have with regard to your future practice of Judaism or your children's upbringing, beyond even the grim statistical prognosis I mentioned, there is the fact that your act itself expresses a profound ambivalence about being Jewish. And it is to that ambivalence that Judaism, or at least a lot of Jews (and not all of them rabbis), will respond.

JL: What fact? Excuse me for saying so, but I decided to marry Annie – that's her name – because we love one another. I suppose if I had spent the last four years in the Ghetto of Greater Pinsk I would have met only Jewish women, but I happen to live in America, where Jews and Christians live together quite happily. In the course of things it seems rather inevitable that Jewish men will meet Christian women (and Christian men Jewish women) and that some of these will fall in love. I guess I would be happier – it certainly would cause fewer problems – if she were Jewish, but it so happens that she isn't. Should that rule the whole thing out? I happen to think marriage is an important enough item for religion not to have automatic veto power over it. If our belonging to different religions really were an issue for either of us, that would be another story; but it's not. And what's true of us is no doubt true of hundreds, maybe thousands, of other couples. You can't expect people to go around overpowering their deepest feelings just because their religions don't match. I hate to sound corny, but I think it's a case of the head not always being able to tell the heart what to do.

AA: Perhaps, if only things were that simple. But my experience in such matters has led me reluctantly to conclude that those two organs are not nearly so distant as people sometimes imagine.

JL: What organs?

AA: Head and heart. Perhaps I am being more candid than I have a right to be. No doubt you came here to get the name of a rabbi to perform this mixed ceremony. But I meant quite literally what I said before about your ambivalence with regard to being Jewish. Certainly you are not so down on the idea that you wish to jettison it entirely. Otherwise there would be no talk of a rabbi: you would be only too happy with your Presbyterian wedding and ham-on-white pastor. And you certainly would not suffer the abusive chidings of your father's friend with your present half-convincing protestations. So there is certainly some part of you that clings to your Jewishness. But the other part, please forgive me for saying so, is not motivated by anything quite so simple as love, at least not if, as seems to be the case, you share the same malady as many American Jews of your generation.

JL: Go on.

AA: You are right that you did not grow up in a Jewish ghetto, which, despite its occasional dangers and indignities, did at least provide a clear picture of the organization of the universe: there were Jews and non-Jews, and a world of difference between. Your universe has been anything but clear: in fact, you have constantly been offered two rather contradictory versions of the significance of your having been born Jewish. America has taught you that Judaism is essentially a religion—one of the three "great" religions in America—and, as the role of religion in American life has generally declined over the last century, the fact that one's religion happens to be Judaism has become increasingly irrelevant. To be a Jew has meant very little in terms of religious practice or outlook or even in terms of one's sense of cohesion with other Jews. For most American Jews, Judaism has been, not so much a religion, something affecting their way of life, as what certain questionnaires used to call "religious affiliation"—that is to say, everybody has one, what's yours? And as the presumption of even a "religious affiliation" has faded and its role in American life diminished utterly, the significance of one's being a Jew has correspondingly dropped to near zero. That at least is the overt message. The covert message is, of course, that being born a Jew can still be a disadvantage. You certainly have not reached the age of twenty or twenty-five without being called a nasty name once or twice, or hearing some anti-Semitic remark, or at least learning of a time in the not too distant past when Jews were held to be somehow undesirable, kept out of the best clubs and universities and professions, if not openly persecuted. Now this combination of messages, the overt and the covert, is deadly. On the one hand, there really is nothing to being Jewish – no religious observance beyond the most perfunctory, no real sense of solidarity with other Jews, not even a sense of one's Jewishness being imposed upon one by a hostile non-Jewish world. At the same time, there is a vague sense of unease, arising at least in part from the realization that, to some Americans, your being a Jew is significant – and, consequently, that hiding one's Jewishness or abandoning it is somehow dishonest, passing oneself off as something one is not. A Jew growing up in such a world is truly in a quandary. He wishes to be honest, to be himself, yet he has no real way of asserting the fact that he is a Jew, other than to say so on the rare occasions when the subject comes up. And, if his name is Judd Lewis, those occasions must be rare indeed, perhaps consisting only of other people making some slightly anti-Semitic remark in his presence on the assumption that he, like them, is a Christian. Isn't that so?

JL: It has happened.

AA: He sees no easy way out of this quandary. He is Jewish, but in a manner of no significance to any but a few random bigots. He feels basically American and utterly at home in America, save for the fact that some Americans still look upon him as somehow other than themselves. It is not a pressing, everyday sort of problem, but it is one connected to his own deep sense of his identity, and, consequently, it is always there, just below the surface of things. But then a solution presents itself to him – or if not quite a solution, at least a step toward easing his problem. If I say "he," by the way, it is because I am talking principally about Jewish young men in America. Not that young women do not also intermarry, but there the motivation is often rather different, less rooted in society at large and more in family relationships.

JL: This all sounds a little psychoanalytical for a confessed banker.

AA: No doubt you're right, but I am almost finished. In any case, his solution is none other than the step you are about to take. For he understands, if not entirely consciously, that marrying his Presbyterian signifies putting to rest his ambiguous situation. Pardon my presumption; perhaps none of this applies to you, in which case I hope you will forgive me for continuing. But there is one telltale gesture that your case shares with a few others I have known. For our Jew, poised as he is to fall into Protestant embrace, has one last quirky demand: he wishes to be married by a rabbi. Of course, he has a half-dozen reasons that he offers for this strange desire. He wants to do it "for his parents" (though often what his parents truly want is that he do nothing of the kind!). His senile grandparents, near death, are not to know that the bride is not Jewish. And so forth. None of these is of any substance. Not even is the idea that he seeks to assert his Jewishness even as he annihilates it quite to the point. Rather, the precise significance of his gesture is this: he wishes, at the very moment that Protestant America embraces him utterly, to be embraced *as a Jew.* Simply to marry the girl would be to go underground, and he feels himself too much a Jew to do that with any honesty. So he must marry her as a Jew, with the rabbi's presence as his certificate, and in so doing symbolically purge his Jewishness of any remaining stigma. Only thus can the fact of his being Jewish become truly incidental, his wife's abiding presence at his side a testimony to its utter insignificance.

JL: Well, that's fascinating, really, if not a little insulting. But tell me, why do you find it so difficult to believe that two people might just fall in love and decide to get married? You concede the fact that being a Jew is largely irrelevant in America, both to the Jews themselves and to non-Jews. So it is for me and Annie. Really, I don't think either of us gave it much of a thought, at least not until we had to plan the wedding. But you insist that this is all only surface, that in some deeper psychodrama I am Judaism's black ram tupping America's white ewe. I suppose anything is possible, but of the two views I must say mine seems by far the more likely.

AA: Well then, why the rabbi?

11

JL: Forget the rabbi, I withdraw the idea. It was stupid to suppose that I could find someone, a rabbi, who would agree with our basic assumption that my being Jewish is, as you say, fundamentally irrelevant. After all, he's paid to think—and act—quite to the contrary.

AA: May I return the bouquet in observing that this is a curiously economic argument for a poet? But if you don't want to listen to me, listen to another writer like yourself, the novelist Philip Roth. He certainly has chronicled what he calls the "Jewish Blues" in America—though sometimes his fiction sounds uncomfortably close to reminiscences, and his writing less like the reflective construction that is art than the raw material usually held to inspire it.

JL: That's not much of a recommendation.

AA: On this particular subject I could recommend no one better. In fact, almost all of his early stories and novels have been about the Jewish-American malady, of which he is clearly an extraordinary sufferer. But he in particular has explored this topic in regard to relations between the sexes—have you read, for example, *Portnoy's Complaint*? A fascinating confession—you really must look at it. There you will find a telling analysis of your generation's situation.

JL: I may not have learned too much in graduate school, but I think I have learned not to confuse a novelist with a sociologist or psychologist.

AA: No doubt you're right, but sometimes I think that a barefoot novelist, whatever else he does, can scout out the truth of a particular time or place long before the armored divisions of social science come rolling in. In any event, all I wished to point out was that Portnoy himself comes to the conclusion that his various non-Jewish loves were not, as you would have it, merely affairs of the heart (though that may have been what he thought at the time), but little social pantomimes. Mind you, I find much of that book wicked and nasty, but this part rings true. And I think that if you interrogate your own heart, and your own history, you may see a connection with your current project. I do not say this with any satisfaction. One could hardly imagine a more personal or idiosyncratic decision than one's choice in marriage. And you are right, it is insulting to imply that such a choice is made for anything other than utterly idiosyncratic and personal reasons. Yet one of those same social scientists, an anthropologist, for example, would surely point out that marriage is first and foremost a social institution, and that this very personal decision is also a public statement addressed to the larger society, a statement about taking one's place within it. It should not strike you as absurd, therefore, that part of your statement in undertaking this marriage concerns your own identity as a Jew, present and future, in that society. And your statement on this is very clearly "yes and no," or rather, "yes, but no."

JL: Hmn.

AA: Nor—though no doubt this will also strike you as insulting—is your "yes, but no" particularly unique. Every weekend the newspapers are full of wedding announcements which, if one reads between the lines, bespeak precisely your problem. Sometimes indeed a "rabbi" even participates in the joint ceremony as you desire. Now it is interesting to observe what sometimes happens after such a marriage is launched. I have heard of more than one case in which, after a time, the non-Jewish wife actually begins to take an interest in Judaism, starts studying Hebrew, and urges the family to attend synagogue. I suppose you might already guess what the husband's reaction to this is.

JL: What?

AA: It is rarely approval. It tends to range from utter indifference to outright hostility, sometimes of a ferocious sort. And, by a certain logic, justifiably so. For it was not "head versus heart" for him, as you say. This man, head and heart, wanted a non-Jewish wife, wanted the social statement that such a match made in America. And now she goes and messes it all up, neutralizes it by becoming one of his own rather than allowing him-and-her together to destroy the categories. No wonder the man gets mad!

JL: I don't know why you keep asserting that Jewish and American are somehow opposed to each other. I certainly don't see them that way, and if a few people in Nebraska or Arkansas do, well, that's their problem. Besides, for me, as you yourself seem to have conceded, Jewish versus American would not be a fair fight. You're a newcomer to America, at least relatively speaking, so perhaps it's natural for you to impose your feelings of differentness on other Jews here. But believe me, we don't feel different. What I *am* is American, down to my fingertips. I feel connected to other Americans—we talk the same way, react the same. . . . In fact, I wouldn't want to advertise it, but if the truth be told I probably have more in common with that Nebraskan anti-Semite than, for example, with a Jew from Israel or even one of those ultra-Orthodox Jews from New York with the black suits and long beards. I'm not particularly happy or sad about it, it's just the way things are, and I certainly don't mean by what I said that I want to deny being a Jew. In fact, I suppose that one of the reasons why I would like to hold on to something Jewish is because the American in me is pretty much swallowing up the Jew whole.

AA: Well, these are slippery items, "American" and "Jewish." You say your ways of talking and thinking mark you overwhelmingly as American. Perhaps; although to be technical about it, there are a few features of your speech—the so-called New York *bring,* for example, or your tendency to turn certain medial *t*'s into plosives—that a trained regional linguist would identify as, if not exclusively Jewish, at least particularly characteristic of Jews in New York and, sometimes, even outside of it. As for your way of thinking, if indeed your reaction *to Jews* is the same as that of the Nebraskan anti-Semite, then there may indeed be cause for worry. But I doubt that this is so. You are an ordinary American Jew, and I will readily concede that that means you have a lot in common with other, non-Jewish Americans. That, however, is not the question. It has been the case of Jews throughout their history—not everywhere, but in quite a few different places—that their speech, their dress, and even, in many respects, their way of thinking have not been distinguishable from those of their non-Jewish neighbors. But I think the question of how one conceives of oneself—or "identity," to use the currently favored, obnoxious term (and one of those, incidentally, whose *t*'s you abnormally plosivize) – turns ultimately not on speech or dress or thought patterns, but, somewhat circularly, on how one chooses to conceive of oneself.

JL: What do you mean? I'm an American not because of what I want to believe, but because I was born here, grew up here, and because – no matter what you say – I talk, walk, think, read, and sleep American. I truly wish I could say the same about the Jewish side of me – but Lewis the Jew seems like gossamer, whereas Lewis the American is brick.

AA: Brick? Perhaps, but as I say, it need not be so. It all depends on your point of view.

JL: What do you mean?

AA: When I look at you, Judd, I see something different from what you see when you look in the mirror. Because you see yourself through American eyes, in that peculiarly American fashion of imagining that each person is no more than himself, made out of thin air, and destined to walk the earth sixty or seventy years, accomplish great things, and then – poof! But what I see is, instead, somebody who was *born*, who came out of his parents and they from theirs, and so on, extending both into the past and into the future – so that a true understanding of who you are, and even of what you will accomplish, must begin with those facts. For that reason I do not see Judd the American at all – or, rather, the fact of your Americanness is simply a late-ish ripple in a long history. I see the son of Jews, themselves the children of Jews, and so on and so on back into Poland or Russia and before that perhaps to Germany, the Rhine Valley, centuries back to the Roman Empire, back even to the time when the Jewish people still lived in their own land.

JL: I think I've heard this speech before. Isn't the last line, "And now you're going to throw it all away"? Only I don't think of marrying Annie as throwing anything away.

AA: Not at all. What I mean is simply that *who you are* is wrapped up in this history, whether you care to see it or not. Nobody comes from

15

nowhere. You are a Jew, a member of this family, and it is only because you happen to live in a society dedicated (for its own ideological reasons) to overlooking people's origins and pretending that they are just homogeneous little bubbles come from nowhere—it is only because of this that this most obvious fact of your being can be hidden from all, even yourself.

JL: It's not that it's hidden, it's just that it's *not that important.* I know where I come from. But that doesn't mean that I'm a member of a tribe or that I'll be struck by lightning if I violate the tribe's marriage taboo. This is the twentieth century, for crying out loud.

AA: Yes, and in the twenty-first century there will be tens of thousands of children, perhaps one or two of them yours, who, now grown up, will be "part Jewish," "have some Jewish blood," or, if the age is less pluralistic than ours, simply "nothing," "Christian." I mean to say that you are a Jew, at least in terms of possibility if not fact. You still could, if you wished, realize that possibility and come to know, really know, what being a Jew can be, come truly to connect with all those generations that have preceded you and—what is more—in some way realize, actualize, this thing that you are but do not yet know. But if, instead, you go ahead with your plans, even that possibility of coming to live fully what you are will be denied to your descendants. Your children will be "half-Jewish" (if that, as I said), theirs will have one Jewish grandparent out of four, and theirs will have nothing at all. Given the increasing longevity of Americans, you may even get to see what the "nothing at all" looks like before you die.

JL: I think we are turning around in circles.

AA: Perhaps.

JL: Despite what you say, I still don't buy the inevitable conflict between Jewish and American. In fact, I don't buy any of what you say. I'm just trying to be what I am, an American Jew who wants to hold on to the Jewish part of me the best I can, starting with my wedding to, admittedly, a woman who isn't Jewish. You may not like it, but those are the facts.

16

AA: Quite candidly, I don't. But my facts don't seem to be getting a much warmer reception than yours.

JL: Namely?

AA: Namely that you're fooling yourself. This marriage is the beginning of the end. Of course it need not be so: if you truly wished, as you claim, to hold on to being a Jew, then at least you might push for your fiancée to convert, instead of cavalierly dismissing the question as some holdover of male domination. Of course, I don't mean to imply that that route would be simple, or even that conversion itself might be easily accomplished—this was one point of my contrast of the large joint-stock corporations of this world to our little Judaism—nor that, in your case, it would solve much: it would simply keep the door open to your becoming, at some point down the road, Jewish in some significant sense. But, as I have said, this is in any case clearly not your desire. So I think under the circumstances that I, we, have a duty at least to speak honestly, Judd. I have known you as long as I have been in this country, and certainly as long as you can remember, and I have great affection for you and your family. But I think that what you are about to do is a mistake, a betrayal of some large part of yourself, and I think that you yourself are aware of it, which is why you try to fool yourself with stories of rabbis at the wedding and a Jewish education for your Christian children. Please forgive my blunt talk, but I really think that there is little more to say.

JL: I guess not.

PART II

(The time: some six months later)

No Generalities

AA: I had some regret in receiving your note, Judd, in spite of what I might have said to you the last time we spoke.

JL: Well, please don't take too much credit for what's happened. I think it mostly belongs elsewhere.

AA: Really?

JL: With her parents, it seems. It turned out that they had somewhat stronger feelings about their daughter marrying a Jew than either she or I had suspected. At least that's what she said. And that apparently got her to reconsidering.

AA: Well, I'm sorry for that. Not, truthfully, that it didn't work out–but it must have been a painful experience.

JL: May I get to the point? As I said in my letter, there were a few things from our last meeting that stayed with me, especially what I took to be an offer to help me learn something more about Judaism . . . if you'd be willing to get me started. I don't suppose what I need should take too long–I really just want an overview, and I'm not a kid, so we don't need to go at a Hebrew school pace. I'd like to discuss things at an adult level.

AA: I would be happy to try, Judd. But I am not so sure it is really possible. Don't you think you would do better to go to the rabbi at your university? Or perhaps there are courses. . . .

JL: Courses are impersonal, and besides, they're about *subjects*; what really interests me is what it means to be religious, I mean, a religious

Jew. That's why I wanted you to help me. Why don't you think you could do it? You've certainly known me a long time, known my family. . . .

AA: To begin with, I am not sure that I would prove a very good teacher, nor you an ideal pupil. I have reflected on this somewhat since receiving your letter. You do have one great advantage, which is that you are a poet. But against this is an even greater disadvantage, that you are an American.

JL: Well, let's have the good news first. Why is being a poet an advantage?

AA: There are two reasons. One is that a poet understands, or should understand, about details, little things, one-time occurrences, as opposed to generalities and frontal assaults. Generalities, in fact, are the great favorite of people in this country, as in Europe too, so that the poet in you will be at war with the American in this matter.

JL: Aren't generalities sometimes useful?

AA: Oh yes – please don't misunderstand. I meant only in relation to understanding the particular thing that you are asking for, what it is to see the world as a Jew. For in the end this must, as you imply, have to do with God, with our reaching out to God. Now quite naturally, you would probably want me to *instruct* you on this subject, to tell you things in some sort of direct fashion. I certainly can appreciate that. But that approach will lead to nothing of value, at least not with me. I'm sure that the university rabbi could do better. . . . With me, in any case, you would have to understand from the beginning that this is not how I can proceed. In fact, you would have to try to do more – you would have to try your best to remove the generality from your mind as a model of proper procedure. Because with this subject, one must proceed entirely differently, with, as I said, little things. You must come to understand that embracing specifics is the only way to move forward. Do you follow me?

JL: More or less.

AA: That other way of thinking, the great general proposition, is characteristic of the world in which we live. In fact, that is a fine phrase for this thinking, "the world in which we live," because in it we conceive of ourselves as inhabiting a generality, we live in a "world," or a country, not far from the capital, part of some amorphous, theoretical nothing. Whereas in fact we inhabit no such place. Yet life moves on by our agreeing to such propositions, indeed, by our reinforcing one another in their acceptance. Imagine, instead, wiping the slate clean, knowing nothing, and then starting to assemble a new knowledge of where we live by moving outward from ourselves inch by inch in the most foreign of territories. Certainly one would never come to encompass America in such a fashion, nor even a small part of it; in fact encompassing—covering territory—would have nothing to do with it. One would seek simply to live in a place and to observe it, not to impose oneself upon it but to allow it, in its fullness, to present itself in time, first this, then this, oh this. That is how you must learn to proceed with the subject at hand. I am speaking about the most basic part. It was not always so, I admit, but it must be so now. You have to start with very little, concrete things, and you must aspire to go no further. That is why I am not sure that we can do this together. And certainly we shall get to no general propositions. But you may come to know certain things, analogous to knowing a certain place, or a certain unnamed glint in the sunlight, not visible all year round, but perhaps in May or August, in midafternoon, or perhaps just on one particular afternoon, *that* afternoon, illuminating, for example, the leaves of a favorite tree in a certain fashion, so that you are provided with a fixed point, a certainty, from which to proceed. Do you see?

JL: To be truthful, I'm not sure that I follow.

AA: You don't see what I mean?

JL: No.

AA: Well, let me try another way, which will be both true in itself, and also an analogy. It is necessary to pray. You must learn to recite the prayer by heart. But you will be eternally frustrated if, in reciting

23

it, you try to imagine its intended Recipient in the manner of your hopeless generalities, or if you observe yourself as if from another set of eyes. What is necessary instead is that you stand before God, nothing less. For this you need great certainty, a firm and familiar path, and the path that you will travel is the path of the prayer. That is why you must memorize it, it must become your backyard. Then your lips and your tongue will travel it like a sure-footed traveler, they will know it—not just the words, but the feel of the words, and in advance—know that just ahead the lips will purse, here the tongue is about to dart back—and these feelings in your mouth will be the certain path. Do you see? They will be the small but sure something.

JL: I think I may understand that. Can you say anything more?

AA: Not yet. Let us talk instead about synagogues.

Three Types of Synagogue

AA: You wish to know another of your disadvantages as an American? It comes from a paradox in the Jewish way. For in Judaism one must begin to know God by seeking to serve God, specifically (as I intimated) the service that our sages called *avodah she-ba-lev,* "the service that is in the heart," that is, prayer. Now one could imagine nothing more intimate or personal than prayer; and yet, for us, prayer is a communal activity, and hardly a spontaneous one. There are set times when people come together to pray to God, on Sabbaths and on weekdays. So although your aim is to know God, you must begin with your fellow human beings, and not only one or two, but a whole group. It is only with them that you can learn to keep the Sabbath and with them that you must say the prayers. Of course, I can get you started with words. But you need to find your group, and in America this is not always easy. You will, alas, have to be on the lookout for three major types of synagogue found in America.

JL: You mean Conservative, Orthodox, and Reform?

AA: No, not these. I am acquainted with the ideologies of these branches of Judaism, as they are called, but from what I have heard, the names do not always tell you what you will actually find when you go inside one of their synagogues. There are, for example, some Conservative synagogues that are almost indistinguishable from Orthodox, and others that seem hardly different from Reform. Besides, as you will see, these "branches" are in any case quite foreign to Jewish history or tradition. No; what I was talking about are three sorts of synagogue a visitor may run into as he tries to find one suitable for himself.

JL: What are they?

AA: The first kind is called the Ceremonial Hall. A Ceremonial Hall is a synagogue that exists principally for the purpose of solemnizing certain occasions and rites of passage—major holidays, weddings, funerals, the thirteenth birthday, and so forth. People "attend" synagogue—a telltale word—on such occasions because, well, these events stir up in them a taste for something ceremonial, and the rabbis who officiate in Ceremonial Halls have, by dint of specialization, developed a certain flair for dealing with significant moments of transition.

JL: Sounds awful.

AA: Perhaps I overstate things. But the distinguishing feature of these places—and one not unrelated to their ceremonial character—is the fact that the congregation is essentially an audience. Their attitude is not very different from that of a crowd in a theater or a moviehouse. Even the most solemn and sacred day of the year, the Day of Atonement—one of the few occasions, by the way, apart from weddings, funerals, and bar mitzvahs, in which the congregation will be represented in full force—loses almost all its significance inside a Ceremonial Hall. I do not know how this came about, but the fact is that the congregation somehow fails to understand the most basic point of the day, that Jews everywhere assemble in order to stand in a multitude before God and ask for forgiveness, so as to start the new year with, so to speak, a clean slate. Instead, the Ceremonial Hall congregation understands the point to be the florid singing of an often overly dramatic cantor, or the rabbi's sermon, to which they listen with the discerning attention of theatergoers marooned in an unwonted matinee. And as they leave they greet vigorously acquaintances not seen since twelve months previous and, after an initial exchange of pleasantries, observe in tones quite reminiscent of a weathered Broadway critic, "He really had it this morning, didn't he?" or "Much better than last year, wasn't it?" or "I'm glad they finally got rid of that last fellow."

JL: That does correspond somewhat to my own experience. I take it there's not much for me there. Let's go on to the other two kinds.

AA: The second kind of synagogue is called the Nostalgia Center. It could not be more strikingly different from the first in appearance. For while the first is generally populated by individuals of somewhat dazzling exterior, businessmen in hand-tailored jackets with bright silk handkerchiefs discreetly peeking out of breast pockets or teenagers in frilly dresses or three-piece suits, the Nostalgia Center's congregation is somewhat shabbier, and it is populated almost exclusively by the elderly. Often, in fact, the rabbi is the youngest person on the premises, and that by some fifteen or twenty years. He is not, however, a performer like the rabbi of the Ceremonial Hall. Rather, his function is that of local authority—despite his youth, he is generally treated with great deference and respect—a figurehead whose arrival signals the time to begin the service. He may or may not himself lead the prayers, save, of course, for the most important part of the Nostalgia Center's liturgy, the Kaddish or memorial prayer for the dead. This is recited in a deliberate, almost painful monotone by the mourners, who each day form a significant percentage of those present and account, alas, for much of the Nostalgia Center's *raison d'être*.

JL: Sounds pretty dreary.

AA: Please don't mistake my purpose. I do not wish to condemn these old, battered institutions, which in another day were vibrant places of assembly. Nor have I said anything about the circumstances that led to their present demise, circumstances that closely reflect the short but tumultuous evolution of Judaism in this country. I simply wish to prepare you for what you will find. And you are right, the Nostalgia Center is a dreary place, the congregants drawn to it out of nostalgic longing for a natural, exuberant Judaism that is no longer theirs, and to its young rabbi as a symbol of the continuity between generations that has in fact eluded them in their own families.

27

JL: Tell me about the third.

AA: The third is rather rarer but definitely on the increase nowadays.

JL: That sounds encouraging.

AA: Perhaps not. For this kind is called the Davening Club. Now, to *daven* (dáh-ven) in Yiddish means to pray. This sort of synagogue consists generally of younger people, some of whom usually have been raised in religious homes observant of Jewish customs. They may have attended Jewish religious schools through elementary or even high school. Sometimes, indeed, they dispense with having a rabbi, because one or more in the congregation is of sufficient education to fulfill all of the functions normally exercised by a rabbi elsewhere.

JL: Sounds fine so far.

AA: It is in some respects an improvement over the other two. Yet even here, I daresay, you will encounter difficulties.

JL: What sort of difficulties?

AA: How can I say. . . . Again, it is that the simplest things are somehow lost, their meaning elusive. For what is a synagogue but a place to come together and stand before God? Yet somehow the Davening Club misses this point. They do not quite pray, they *daven,* the latter word becoming, in their transformation of it, a merely human interaction, a recitation destined only for each other's ears. For the same reason it is called a club, for its activities in general are not directed upward, but only to the well-being of its own members. As I mentioned, they sometimes lack a rabbi, but this is often quite by design, for they themselves enjoy taking turns at fulfilling the rabbi's functions, preaching sermons to each other or running educational classes.

JL: In the end it doesn't sound much better than the first two.

AA: I have not wanted to discourage you. On the contrary. My whole reason for explaining about these three kinds was to help you understand that none of them is truly worthy of the name of synagogue. They are a strange aberration, or, rather, three aberrations that for some reason seem to have sprouted up in America.

JL: But America is where I live. If none of the three kinds is any good, where am I supposed to go?

AA: Well, certainly, these are not all that you will find here. There are many fine places I know of, quite a few, really, and if you are persistent, you eventually will find the one that is right for you. As for these three types—well, frankly, I am at a loss to explain them. You know, American Jews are extraordinary. They have achieved so much in such a short time—I don't just mean individually, but as a community as well. They truly have a genius for communal organization that is quite unmatched in Jewish history, and their institutions are a monument to hard work and self-sacrifice. But, on the other hand, something seems to have been lost in the process, or at least in the congregations that I have described. Perhaps you will be able to explain it better than I can. But sometimes it seems that the most basic things, things that you could find in any backwater little *minyan* in the Orient, are here as precious as pearls. And so you must look hard for your group.

But part of my point in this catalogue was precisely to say that even synagogues such as those I describe have something to offer you, and you must learn to take the best from them. For no matter how they may function as a group, these congregations do contain individuals—certainly the rabbi if no one else—from whom you may learn and then, if it is necessary, move on. The point is, you have far to go, and time is short. It is wise to learn, as our Rabbis said, from each person whatever he can teach you.

JL: Excuse me, but I'm not quite sure why you're talking about *other* teachers. I was hoping that you might be the one to give me some kind of crash course—maybe not teach me everything, but enough to get me started on my own.

AA: Well, I certainly can say a few more things to get you started. But to know what the Sabbath is—or Shabbat, as we call it in Hebrew—you must live it and see it from within a Jewish family that

29

keeps it. And the prayers—well, you must first learn some Hebrew in order to say them in Hebrew, but you must also learn the manner in which they are spoken and sung, the little tunes, and such things you will only learn in the synagogue itself. And, as I said, it is in any case proper at certain times to pray as part of a group. Likewise the study of Jewish texts: studying in our sense is not like studying in the university—it is a religious activity, done not to arrive at something but simply for its own sake. And again, this is done ideally with someone else. That is why finding the right group is so important.

JL: You'll have to admit that the situation does not sound very inviting. First you tell me how depressing synagogues are in America —

AA: Some of them, true, but only some —

JL: Then you go on to insist that they are somehow essential to my learning about Judaism.

AA: As I said, my aim was principally to help you to understand that such congregations are not what a synagogue is supposed to be. But I think that if you are willing to look around, you will find individuals, and ultimately a group, that may suit you.

JL: You don't make it sound very easy.

AA: I am sure that it is not. And believe me, I have not forgotten what ultimately it is that you are aiming for, however distant from it some of what I have mentioned may seem. But this is the Jewish path, and you must walk it as others have. And it is not as long as it might now seem. In a few months you will be well along, and in a year you will be quite at home. But you must begin by finding your group, your *first* group anyway.

JL: To be perfectly frank, I'm not sure I want to start looking for my group, as you call it. I may not have spent a lot of time in synagogues, but I think your description only confirms my own impression, and it's in spite of that impression that I came to you. You're the only person I know who seems—I hate to put it this way—both religious, I mean in terms of Judaism, and, well, willing to talk about it, intelligently I mean. You see, I'm not interested in being missionized by my local rabbi or even joining some study group. I'm most of all interested in finding out what it is to "understand the world as a Jew," as you put it, to see things the way you see them. And that includes, of course, what it means to believe in God, although that is something I really don't know about.

AA: Of course. But I said before that I might turn out to be less than the ideal teacher, and this is what I meant. I wish I could explain what I see in your terms, but I know of no way. There is a verse in the Psalms that well expresses the problem. It says, " I would rather stand at the threshold of God's house than reside in the dwellings of evil." At first the verse seems quite pointless—for, given a choice between God's house and the "dwellings of evil," who would not prefer the former? But the point is that "standing in the threshold" is far less than "residing," far less than settling down and leading one's life; and so the psalmist is saying that in spite of all that, I would still choose the halfway existence, the no-life of standing at the threshold, if it is the threshhold of Your house, over living even sumptuously outside of it, that is, in "dwellings in evil." Now standing in the threshold of God's house is, in a sense, what you are asking me to do—to stand at a point that is neither truly inside nor outside, but from which I can both glance within and yet still converse with one who stands outside, describing to him in his language what he cannot see. Perhaps there are people who can do this, but I am not one. The only solution, I think, would be for you to walk through the door with me and, little by little, take stock of what is inside yourself.

JL: But what does it mean to "walk through the door"?

The Mishkan

AA: The cliché about Judaism is still true: it is not so much a religion as a way of life. And the way to "walk through the door" is to begin to adopt that way of life, to keep the Sabbath and our festivals and say the fixed prayers every day, to observe our laws of pure food and of proper behavior, and in all ways to try to act like a Jew.

JL: But how can someone begin to do any of those things without first having the basic framework? How can you begin to say prayers to a God that you're not at all sure about in the first place?

AA: Isn't it this way with children who grow up in a Jewish home? Long before they can properly understand, in fact, almost before they can talk, they are taught the difference between the Sabbath and the rest of the week, that certain things are done only in the one and not in the other; and shortly after they speak their first words they begin to learn the words of blessing that we say before eating this or that kind of food or washing our hands before a meal. The understanding of God, if any, that may accompany these acts is, of course, perfectly childish, but what does it matter? Because a *place for understanding* is opened up inside the children by their doing these things, and that place will be filled with greater and greater insight as they go on.

JL: But what if the person starting out is already grown up?

AA: Nevertheless, the path is the same. It is often pointed out that, in the Torah, when God proposes to the people of Israel to become their God – a state of affairs that will mean adopting His Torah and its laws – the people are said to have answered with one accord, *"Na'aseh venishma'.*" The Hebrew words mean something like, "Let us do and obey." But the second word (more literally "hear" or "heed") has another meaning in Hebrew, "to understand." And so our Rabbis interpreted this response as "Let us do and let us [then] understand," asserting that *doing* properly precedes understanding, and that in fact it is sign of merit if one undertakes to serve God even before understanding what this means. And this is true whether one is a child or an adult (for the Israelites were a whole nation at the time these words were spoken, men and women of all ages as well as children). One must begin by doing.

JL: It seems a little strange.

AA: No doubt it does, but this strangeness is in part connected to that peculiarly American difficulty I mentioned earlier. You want to understand everything before learning anything. There is no progress possible with such a mentality. But if I say that there is a certain order in which things are to be done, it is because without following the order you would not appreciate even the greatest knowledge; it would seem trivial to you or pass without notice.

JL: Why is that?

AA: Perhaps one might say that it is somewhat analogous to passing suddenly from a very dark place, a sealed-off closet to which one's eyes have become accustomed, into a brightly illuminated room. One is, of course, aware of the change in lighting, but to the room itself and what it contains one is temporarily blinded. The analogy is imperfect, but you can see that by moving in stages from darkness to light, one can prepare one's eyes before entering the bright room and so be able to take in and appreciate what one encounters.

JL: Why is the analogy imperfect?

AA: I have presented it in this fashion because light is what makes seeing possible and (since seeing is a form of perception) it is usually associated metaphorically with knowledge, "enlightenment," "illumination," and so forth, whereas darkness is connected in our minds with all that is obscure. Yet I confess that in thinking about the reality

33

that I am attempting to describe, it has seemed to me that it might be better to present the transition in quite the opposite fashion, as of a person moving from a brightly illuminated room to a darker one, one lit only with ordinary, natural light.

JL: What's the difference?

AA: To me at least, the brightly illuminated room suggests the everyday garish reality in which people generally exist, their lives a colorful pantomime played out in primary hues and accompanied by the blaring music of the quotidian. In such a state they tend to forget that the lighting of the room is artificial, and that what seems to look one way is often simply the effect of brash fluorescence on surfaces, a *trompe l'oeil.* Cut the electricity, however, and the same space will take on an utterly different look. Perhaps, if there is now some daylight in the room, the eyes will not be blinded by the change, as in the first analogy. But everything they see will now have a different aspect, a different message, the garishness having been replaced by all the subtle and infinitely detailed play of ordinary daylight on the things of this world. This change—from garish fluorescence to what is natural and quite real—more closely corresponds to the change I am describing. But, to pursue the analogy, people at first will not appreciate such a change—they will be disturbed by the sudden dimness (so it will seem) and cry, "Lights!" "What happened to the electricity?" and so forth, unless they have been properly prepared.

JL: I think I see. But it's still hard for me to imagine that the things you mentioned, keeping the Sabbath and the others, could have the effect you describe.

AA: To do these things is, as I said, to open up a space, a possibility in our hearts and in our lives that would otherwise remain closed. Without such a possibility, we are simply overcome by ourselves and can go nowhere.

JL: Overcome by ourselves?

AA: Yes, because we are big. About this we shall speak some other time. But for now you must understand that the way to begin is by doing: this is the Jewish way and always has been.

JL: Doing what? I mean, besides going to synagogue regularly.

AA: Synagogue has little to do with it, though this is a common misconception. But the "doing" of Judaism, whether with regard to the Sabbath or the rest of the week, takes place at home and at work much more than in the synagogue. For our way is to seek to connect all the little details of our lives with the specifications of the Torah, and we do this from the moment we wake up to the moment we fall asleep. The most trivial actions, from opening one's eyes in the morning to washing one's hands or tying one's shoes or walking out the door, are all done in a special way. A Jew does not start to eat or drink the slightest thing without first saying certain words. And so throughout the day, whatever else we may be doing, our thoughts and our deeds are continually being directed upward. But more than that, what we actually do in a given day is to some extent determined or governed by Jewish laws and customs. So, for example, it is our way to undertake certain actions, such as to study a little portion of our books each day and to help the needy by giving charity daily and similar acts. We will likewise seek to avoid certain things in our daily relations, such as cheating or anger or hypocrisy, as well as not to eat certain foods, and to avoid yet other specific things forbidden in the Torah. And so, even as we go about our daily routine, we are always trying to fulfill the things specified in the Torah and to direct our actions appropriately. And beyond even this are the set times devoted to our religion. Besides the Sabbath and holy days such as Rosh ha-Shanah and Kippur and Passover, there are the fixed times during the weekday world. Three times a day, in fact, morning, afternoon, and night, we put aside what we are doing in order to stand and say silently the words of a prayer, the one I spoke of before. Ideally this is done in a group, and there are many Jews who go to the synagogue each day in order to do so. But it is also quite proper to pray alone, and so there are Jews all over the world who set aside fifteen minutes or half an hour for the morning prayer before they leave their houses for work and again some few minutes in the late afternoon and evening for those other prayers.

JL: Do you? I mean, do you do all the things you mentioned?

AA: Oh yes. This is our way of living, our *halakhah*.

JL: I'm surprised that you can find the time.

AA: It is not so much a matter of time: the time is there to be taken. But this way of living consists not only of those minutes of the day or week that are specifically given over to one duty or another, but also of the rest of the time, which is changed because of them.

JL: I'm not sure I understand.

AA: It is as I said: the purpose is to open up a space, a possibility, in the heart. Once the opening is made, it can be filled. Let me explain it in the terms set forth by the Torah itself. After the people of Israel had been led out of Egypt and slavery, God ordered them to build for Him a certain structure, called in Hebrew *mishkan*. This word is usually translated as "tabernacle" or "tent," but its basic meaning is simply "dwelling," a place of residence. Now to us this demand might at first seem strange; after all, as Scripture says elsewhere, the heavens themselves cannot contain God, and all of earth (it notes with perhaps a smile) is like a little stool on which He might, as it were, put up His feet—why then command the Israelites to build this tiny little tent as His *mishkan*? Moreover, why should *they* build it—could not the Creator of the universe have chosen some magnificent feature of the natural world that He had fashioned in which to, as it were, dwell, rather than relying on merely human artisans? But the point was, as I said, for them to open up a space in order to allow Him to fill it. And this is the most basic principle of our way, to open up such a space in our lives and in our hearts. Then such a space will have the capacity to radiate outward. So the holiness of the *mishkan* radiated out to fill the whole camp of the Israelites during their wanderings, and the camp itself became changed as a result. And it was quite proper that the people be the ones to build God's dwelling, because this is the way it always must be: the people create the space and then God can fill it.

36

JL: It really sounds to me like some kind of psychological process —

AA: It is no more psychological than building the *mishkan,* which was done (as the Torah tells in loving detail) with real boards and bronze clasps and linen curtains.

JL: Exactly, whereas what you are talking about is saying prayers and not eating certain foods —

AA: It is the same. It is also a structure, very much a structure, a pattern of actions, and one that keeps open the heart in the same fashion. Perhaps this sounds to you like an empty metaphor. But as I am speaking to you I can see it vividly in my mind. So long as the inside of you remains unbreached, you might be standing at the entrance of the holiest part of that *mishkan,* yet you would still be quite blind to God's presence, because there would be no place inside you in which to receive the impression. But once that smooth surface of the heart has been opened up, a little place in it opened and shored up to stay open, then God's radiance can enter and radiate outward within you; then you could not bear to stand in that same spot of the *mishkan,* so great is the radiance, but would flee to the outer parts.

Our early rabbis expressed this same principle in just these terms. For the *mishkan,* after some period of use in Jewish history, was ultimately replaced by the great Temple in Jerusalem; then for centuries and centuries this Temple was God's dwelling in Israel. When it was destroyed in war in the year 70 of the common era (that is, 70 "A.D."), the people felt an enormous loss, for the great physical space that had been hollowed out in the nation's midst was now profaned, its ceremonies and worship put to an end by an alien invader. This was, and remains, a great lack. Yet one of our Rabbis from early times, the teacher Ulla, put it well when he said, "From the time that the Temple was destroyed, God has had naught on earth but the four cubits of *halakhah.*" The expression "four cubits" in Hebrew means a minimal distance or area, a few square feet. But what did he mean by comparing *halakhah,* our way of life, that is, all the practices of Sabbaths and weekdays, prayers and proper foods and the other things I mentioned, with a physical structure, the Temple? You yourself started to say how different two such things are. Yet in another way, they are the same, as Ulla meant it. For just as the Temple constituted a space, a possibility, so does our *halakhah* constitute a space. Perhaps compared to the Temple, our *halakhah* seems modest, four cubits as opposed to a magnificent edifice. Yet his point was that both are structures, both serve to open up a space, so that even with the loss of the great physical space of our Temple, God's presence was not denied a place in Israel: each Jew carried the possibility of opening a space within his or her own heart and life. And so it is today. The trick is to start to construct and so to open.

JL: Is the process of opening a space gradual?

AA: The space is always made by human beings and can be made quickly or slowly. But when God fills the space it is always quick and never gradual.

JL: Can God open up the heart even if it has no prepared space?

AA: Of course. But the space itself makes for a permanence, a constant possibility, rather than something fleeting. And so the Torah speaks of "circumcising" the heart in just this fashion, altering it permanently and beyond recall.

JL: And how does one begin to make the space? Just start doing all the things that you said?

AA: You can start all, or you can start one. Perhaps it is better to start with one.

JL: Which is that?

AA: The Sabbath, this is the first. Not that there is strictly speaking a first or second, but the Sabbath might be considered the beginning, as is even hinted at in our Torah, which mentions the Sabbath right at the start, in its account of the creation of the world.

Shabbat

JL: What does it mean to keep the Sabbath?

AA: Shabbat has two sides to it that might at first seem opposites. On the one hand it is a day that is set aside as holy—*shabbat kodesh,* we say, the holy Sabbath—and as such it is deemed to belong to God, for this is what "holy" means in Judaism, set aside as belonging to God. Indeed, it is a principle of our Torah that since all things are given to us by God, we seek to return a part to Him in recognition of this fact. So part of the new harvest was set aside as God's and offered at the Temple in Jerusalem, and the firstborn of the herds and flocks are similarly consecrated. The case of the Sabbath is similar: we are given seven days of the week, but one of these we seek to give back to God. And we do this by not doing the things we normally do on the other six days, not practicing our professions or doing any work whatsoever.

JL: Then what is the other aspect of Shabbat?

AA: From what I have said so far, you might think that the day would be an austere occasion, given over to fasting and religious self-denial. But the truth is quite the opposite: it is a happy time, the highlight of the week, and Jews all over the world look forward to Shabbat as a haven and respite from the workaday world. To keep Shabbat means to have one day of the week that is completely special, so special that it towers above all the other days of the week, until the other days seem to exist only for the sake of Shabbat. On Shabbat one leaves aside one's weekday being and so becomes, virtually, a different person, or, you might say, becomes more truly oneself. As for food, not only is it not a fast day, it is in fact an institutionalized feast: one

39

is required to do what one can in order to have three substantial meals on Shabbat, with the best foods of the week, and even wine. And since cooking is one of the forms of work that are forbidden and all the meals must therefore be prepared in advance (though, in pre-scribed fashion, they can be heated up again), the only Sabbath "duty," as far as food is concerned, is to eat and drink what has been prepared. As with food, so with other things: it is a day when all the normal little tasks have been outlawed in order to make the peaceful-ness and rest that much more complete.

But what I have said is really only the barest outline. I cannot tell you in words what it means to keep Shabbat, and especially to live in a community of people who do the same—the songs at the table and the special foods, the special way of doing everything—and the fact that all this is intended first of all as an expression of the love of God and the desire to live according to the Torah—someone who does not know Shabbat in this fashion certainly does not know what it is to be a Jew. Nor, for that matter, can you understand what our holidays are without living them—the preparations before Pesah, the songs that we sing only then, or what it is like to sit outside in the homemade *sukkah* on a fall afternoon, and so forth. Perhaps most of all, you can-not now understand how the rest of the week is changed by Shabbat or the whole rhythm of the year is shaped by our festivals. But if you could know these things, you would see how poor and empty is a life in which they are absent.

JL: But what about all the things that you're *not* allowed to do?

AA: Well, I have just given you a bare summary. Because "not work-ing" is really a full-time preoccupation on Shabbat. It does not just mean not going to work. Here the comparison with the *mishkan* may be helpful, because in Shabbat what we aim to do is to create an open space in the clearest sense: we empty our lives of the workaday world. This means not only not going to work or doing work at home, but not driving a car or going shopping or watching the television, in fact, not doing most of the little things that, whether we realize it or not, compose a good bit of our weekday existence. As a matter of fact, we do not even turn electric lights on or off or answer the telephone.

JL: But who decides these things? I know that Orthodox Jews don't answer the phone on Saturdays, but I can't imagine that it says not to in the Torah. How could that be an issue before telephones were invented?

AA: It could not. The basic principles of Shabbat are contained in the Torah, but even in biblical times it was necessary to spell out their implications in more specific fashion. Thus, for example, the Torah prohibits "doing work"–the biblical phrase really means doing a "profession"–but what did it mean? If one abstained from doing one's own profession, was it permitted to practice someone else's–that is, could a farmer fix his roof or a roofer tend his garden? Elsewhere the Torah says that one may not "kindle a fire" on the Sabbath–but was it permitted to light a fire beforehand and allow it to continue burning into the Sabbath?

JL: It sounds like these should all be matters of individual interpretation. There may not necessarily be one right or wrong answer.

AA: But there had to be.

JL: Why? If the point is to make the Sabbath a day of rest, why not let everyone go about it as best he or she can?

AA: There are two reasons. First of all, the Sabbath was an obligation on the community as a whole. In fact, one of the duties imposed by the Torah was to enforce the laws of Shabbat and punish members of the community who violated them. You're right that much in this comes to a matter of interpretation and did so even in the biblical period. Such interpretations and clarifications were taught, alongside the written text of the Torah, from earliest times. But the point is this: the precise meaning and application of biblical laws like the Sabbath had to be clear and universally accepted if the community was to fulfill its duty to enforce the law. And, I might add, to have the whole community keeping the Sabbath in the same way was–again, in a way that it is difficult for modern people to understand–a given, understood by itself.

JL: What was the second reason?

AA: It was, and is, simply that to make the Sabbath a general requirement whose details might be left to individual discretion would be to make a weak structure, in fact, no structure at all. Because it is in this as in all things: the more specific, the stronger. At first it might not seem so. For there is something rather noble sounding in talking about a day of rest, and that nobility seems, if anything, diminished by our then getting down to the practicalities of telephones and electric lights, what sort of electric timer may be used to turn on lights automatically, or under what circumstances a refrigerator may be opened. In reality, however, it is the little details that are blessed. And again, the Torah tells us as much with regard to the *mishkan*. For God's commandment could have been, simply, "Build me a magnificent structure and I will dwell in it." Instead, He spelled out all the specifics – the size of the boards and the precise number, the kind of wood to be used, how the clasps were to connect things, what was to be of gold, of silver, of purple, and so on and so forth, chapter after chapter of little details. It is because each of these is a blessing and a source of strength. Then, after all the details are given (and it is, as I said, a matter of many pages), the Torah turns around and recounts, detail by detail again, how each of these specifications was actually carried out. Now here is a further, and telling, point. For if the Torah's aim in listing all these specifics – and not only of the *mishkan* and its appurtenances, but also all the details of the robes to be worn by the priests who were to serve there – were simply to give us an exact picture of what was to be, certainly one listing of all these particulars would have been sufficient. Their repetition points to another purpose. It is not only to say that the whole strength of the *mishkan* lay in these very details, but to highlight the importance of the proper observance of God's specifications precisely in regard to those details. "Build me a structure, any old structure" would not, in the terms we have been using, have hollowed out a strong space, and the pressure from the outside might have collapsed its walls. But each particular strut and curtain, by being named, made the whole stronger, and it was in carrying out such details precisely that the people were able to find success. So too, Shabbat is a matter of little details, and the fact that they are one way and not another is what allows its walls to be strong and the space's integrity to be maintained.

"This Is My God"

JL: I'm sure I can get to understand the rules. But I'm still not sure I see how knowing any of this is going to amount to being very, well, important.

AA: And what is important?

JL: Well, if someone is going to pursue a particular path, as you say, it seems to me that what's attractive, ultimately, is how it changes your perception of things, how it brings you to something new, some kind of enlightenment, really. I mean, there are Zen Buddhist monks who meditate fourteen hours a day or who end up contemplating a particular mountain for twenty years, or Sufi ecstatics, or other contemplative and mystical traditions. Next to these, the haggling about what is or isn't permitted on Shabbat seems, pardon my saying so, rather petty. I mean, if Shabbat is, as you say, a day given over to God, then why even talk about shortcuts and what *might* be allowed? Forget the electric timers and refrigerators and everything and make it a whole day of meditation or prayer or whatever. I know there's a mystical side to Judaism—in fact, isn't that what the Kabbalah is all about, Jewish mysticism? That's the part that really attracts me, much more than what is or isn't permitted on Shabbat. As a matter of fact, that's what I expected we'd be talking about. I'd be happy to spend all of Shabbat at home in the dark and eat only bread for lunch if it was really going to lead to something, something basic.

AA: You are right that there are elements in Judaism, especially in what is called Kabbalah, that are in some ways similar to what is called mysticism elsewhere. But you are wrong to think that the petty particulars in the laws of Shabbat are a side issue or somehow not crucial (they are, I might add, crucial to just those Kabbalists, among others). They may not look it, but these laws, with their setting down of precise definitions and everyday examples, are no less than the struts and props of the *mishkan*. They are the blessed details. I do not know what it means to be a Buddhist, but I can tell you that Judaism is about the service of God, and that service consists precisely of blessed details. Because an idea, such as "contemplating ultimate reality" or "God is love," will not go far on its own. It needs legs, which is to say, it needs *halakhah*. That is why, when the Torah speaks of "loving" or "fearing" God, it adds, "keeping His commandments," or sometimes "keeping His commandments, His laws, and His ordinances." These are the legs, these are what turn an idea into a way of life. And this, it seems to me, is the great strength of Judaism. For with us, when a person wishes to reach out to God, the desire will not simply come and go in the heart, a fleeting feeling. But we have a structure for our daily lives so that that desire can take form, many different forms, and these will all be able to carry the desire and even strengthen it in the process, so that it returns and returns, until our lives themselves become a kind of reaching out.

JL: Yes, but isn't there the same kind of structure, and fixity, in other systems? After all, people who meditate do it a certain number of minutes or hours a day, or even continuously, as I mentioned. There's certainly structure in that—and it's strong, it produces results. I mean, people who meditate talk about how it gives them something like inner peace or changes their ordinary perception of things. It seems to me that that's what every religion is ultimately about. Doesn't Judaism, or the Kabbalah at least, give you something like that, some kind of changed perception? I mean you, personally.

AA: As I said, Judaism is about serving God, about offering up our thoughts and everyday actions to God. So you are wrong from the start about what Judaism gives us. Judaism gives us *to* God. And this too is a profound difference between our *halakhah* and these other things you mention. Of course, I have only observed them as an outsider, so perhaps I misjudge them. Yet it seems to me that so much of

44

the appeal that meditation and the like have for Americans is precisely that they promise to deliver, to reward steady effort with peace of mind, altered consciousness, and so forth. Nothing could be farther from Judaism. And the fact that their orientation seems to me ultimately so far from the heart and from what is real makes it hard for me to imagine that there is anything of substance to them. Their approach seems more like a kind of spiritual jogging, guaranteed to lower the heartbeat and make you a happier, all-around human being.

JL: But I'm not sure—maybe you're right, Americans are just different. . . . I'm not sure, in any case, I could ever see things in terms of "the service of God." And I wish I could be like the Jews who said, "Let's do now and understand later." But I think, frankly, I'd feel a little silly about doing these things on Shabbat without having resolved some of the larger issues first. To begin with, some of the Eastern systems of thought and meditation don't even have a concept corresponding to the notion of God—they're more about "energy" or "change," and it's my impression that modern physics in curious fashion has come to some of the same conclusions. And certainly it is difficult for modern people to get into the idea of some kindly Old-Man-in-the-Sky watching over humanity's fortunes.

AA: Don't be foolish.

JL: I beg your pardon?

AA: No doubt children, or even adults who still stand on the outside, may imagine things in such terms. But that is only because they have not yet understood. The truth is there for you to grasp. But in Judaism, understanding emerges from within a framework consciously put into place, and this, for the reasons I have stated, is quite as it should be. You know, in several places the Torah speaks of "learning to fear God." No expression might at first seem stranger than this one. Yet it occurs, as I say, at least four or five times. And each time the point is the same: that one does indeed *learn*, and that the way to learn is by doing the things that are prescribed in the Torah. This is the framework.

JL: Yes, but certainly even to enter into the framework you have to believe, or at least entertain the belief, in God. Without that there's nothing, right?

AA: Yes.

JL: Well that's just the problem. How does someone go about bringing himself to believe something that he really has no personal basis for believing?

AA: There are several ways in which I could answer you. But I think the best and most direct would be this: In the heart there are many things that are hidden from view. You are worried about believing in God. Let me tell you, you must not worry. Let me tell you: you already believe in God. Your heart knows this, and that is why you came here. But now you are struggling with nets and cables, with the world as you have been taught to understand it without God. That is why you must put those things aside, not fight them, just hold them in reserve. They will come back some day. But for now you have to go inside, into the small world of real things, and give freedom to your heart. This is how you will discover what you already believe and what you must do.

JL: And how do I do that?

AA: But I have already told you. You must give freedom to your heart and let it lead you. Then the way of our *halakhah* will invite you. Our Rabbis put it well when they taught, "Everything is in God's hands save for the fear of God." They meant that the "fear" of God—that is, belief in God and the desire to serve God—is in human hands, a willingness to give the heart its freedom. I admit, it is a frightening step, all the more because you do not even know where you are going.

JL: What do you mean?

AA: Accepting what our Rabbis called "the yoke of God's kingship" and the duty of the commandments is not a step one can really understand in advance. You take it in the dark. In fact, it is interesting that more than once the Torah seems to show that, no matter how a person has been brought up or prepared, the reality of God always surprises him, even overwhelms him, when he at last stands in God's presence.

JL: How so?

AA: For example, when the people of Israel turned to God and were freed from Egypt, the Torah tells us that the Egyptians pursued them to the edge of the Red Sea. There the sea parted and they were miraculously saved. Now about this account our ancient Rabbis observed that the lowliest of our people was in that instant raised up to a level of communion with God higher even than that of a prophet. This observation was based on what the people say at that moment, as they look back over the sea and their salvation: "This is my God and I will praise Him." It is, our Rabbis said, as if each and every Jew at that instant could perceive God so near as to be able to say, "This."

JL: I understand.

AA: Not yet. Because the full verse is as follows: "This is my God and I will praise Him, the God of my father and I will glorify Him." That particular moment was not only one of proximity, it was one of recognition as well. For, of course, the Jews had been instructed about "the God of my father"; they had been told all about their own ancestors and the God worshiped by Abraham, Isaac, and Jacob. But this remained—as it must always—history, description. It was only at the Red Sea that they could say, out of their very lives, "This is my God," and then add, in the surprise of recognition, "and the God of my father as well."

JL: Are you saying that all people, at one point or another, are destined to stand at their own "Red Sea"?

AA: Don't be silly. I am speaking to you, and what I am saying is that no amount of talking about reaching out to God will tell you very much. Let me see if I can show you in another way—though it would certainly help if you knew Hebrew, and knew the Torah. But

47

the same is true of Moses himself, at the beginning of the book of Exodus, when, having fled the Egypt of his youth, Moshe, Moses, comes to settle in Midian. When God calls to him out of the burning bush, Moses is at first both reverent and curious—but it is also clear that he does not truly understand what it is all about. (In a way, he is like yet another prophet, Samuel, whom God has to call four times before the poor fellow can know that the voice he is hearing is not a human one, but God's—but that is another story and each human being is in any case different.) With Moses, God tells him, in rather long and intimidating fashion, that he must return to Egypt to save the Israelites. Moses refuses, he says that he is unable. But the phrase he uses is revealing: "Who am I to go to Pharaoh and take the Israelites out of Egypt?" *Who am I*—because, since the voice is heard in his heart, he does not fully understand its significance and so turns the discussion to himself. And so God answers him in kind. "But I will be with you," He says. Moses still does not understand, but continues on, "Suppose I *do* go to the Israelites and say to them, 'The God of your fathers has sent me to you,' then they will say, 'What is His name?' What can I tell them then?" It seems, perhaps, that Moses was offering what salesmen like to call a "dangler," the kind of objection a customer makes when he is interested but unsure: "If X were so, I might consider your offer, but as it is now, I can't." This is very much the answer that Moses gives: "I'm not saying that I would do it even if I did know your Name, but the fact is I don't, so the whole thing is out of the question." The purpose of a dangler is to bargain, sometimes only for time, in which case the dangler's point is often quite irrelevant as stated. And indeed, would God's *name* be the sort of thing that the people would ask about after such a declaration? No, it is Moses who wants to know God's name, because here he stands at the turning and is suddenly perplexed about his Interlocutor. God's answer is equally telling. For on the surface what he says to Moses is, politely, "Mind your own business." Yet the way in which this is phrased in Hebrew is quite remarkable: "I am who I am." To the one whose first question was, "Who am I to go to Pharaoh . . . ?" He then answers still more directly, and says, "Thus shall you say to the Israelites, 'I am' has sent me to you." Do you wish to know who you are to go to Pharaoh? Then this is your answer, and the one that you will bring back to your people. And lest there be any mistake, God then repeats the same instruction in different form: "Thus shall you say to the Israelites: The Lord, the God of your fathers, the God of Abraham, the God of Isaac, and the God of Jacob has sent me to you. This is my name forever, and that is how I am called in every age." Do you follow me?

JL: Not really.

AA: "This name" and "that" one in Moses' mouth here are like "This is my God" and "the God of my father" for the Israelites at the Red Sea. Now, you wish to reach out to God, and so you must do it. And you are partway there, because the wish itself comes from your heart. But you must open your heart, build it open with the *mishkan* as I have said, and forget about ideas and descriptions because these are general, not untrue but belonging to "the God of my father." But you must go further, for the sure, small particulars.

The Shema

AA: There is another matter that I should mention, one that is connected to this one. Because, beside Shabbat, there is one *mitzvah,* one commandment, that you should undertake to begin right away. It is the saying of the *Shema,* the reading of three special paragraphs from the Torah in the morning and evening.

JL: Is this another thing that people do every day?

AA: You mean you've never heard of *Shema Yisrael?*

JL: No, I've heard of it, in fact I memorized it once, but the words never really did make much sense to me. Isn't it, "Hear O Israel, the Lord our God, the Lord is One"?

AA: That is one way of translating, but I suppose I would agree that in such a form the words might be difficult to understand.

JL: Well, how should they be translated?

AA: They really address the same point we saw before. You see, God is spoken of with different names in the Torah. In some places the Torah uses the general name, *Elohim,* which is like our word "God." But elsewhere it uses a special name, one that we never pronounce because of its holiness. This was the name that was revealed to Moses, and whose sound is similar to the "I am" that God spoke to him. In English this special name is usually translated as "the Lord," because in Hebrew we say in its place *Adonai,* "my Lord."

JL: Why should the Torah use two names?

AA: There are many explanations for this. But what is important here is to explain the sense of the *Shema*. Of course, you cannot really understand all of what I am saying now, but perhaps you will remember the words and understand them later on. The name *Elohim* is, as I said, a general name. At the time when the Torah was given, many of Israel's neighboring peoples referred to their gods by the same name—indeed, the Torah itself speaks of "gods," *elohim,* made of wood and stone, that is, idols. It was a term common to everybody and expressed primarily a relationship. If we were to compare this matter to a situation in daily life, we might say that it is like a little child growing up who calls his father "Daddy." This too expresses a relationship, and there are many daddies, even though he only has one. But then at a certain point the child becomes aware that the father has another name, one that is his alone. This name does not express a relationship but is a unique form of reference. So is it in Hebrew with these two names.

JL: And so?

AA: The "relational" name can be understood, as it were, from the outside: we all know what it is for a child to call someone "Daddy," what sort of a relationship that implies, and this is true as well for the relationship implied by "God." Yet such a name tells us nothing about the nature of the One so addressed. And so indeed, when we are taught about God, or hear about God, what we understand is the relationship. This is, so to speak, "the God of my father," the one I was told about. But then there comes a time when we are ready to know more than the relationship, when we are ready to know God, as it were, by name—not to speak the name, or necessarily even to think of it, but to reach out to God in particular, to know specifically Him. Only when that happens is it possible to understand fully the words of the *Shema*. But try to remember this for later. What the words mean is more like, "Understand this, people of Israel: the Lord—that is, God-in-particular—is our God; He is the only one."

JL: I see.

AA: Perhaps not, but I hope that you will. In the meantime what you must do is to get yourself your own prayerbook (*siddur*, as it is now called) and learn to say the whole *Shema* every morning and evening. Because the *Shema* does not consist of just this one sentence but, as I mentioned, of three separate paragraphs, taken from three different places in the Torah. It takes a few minutes to say them, even when you know the whole thing by heart. Later, you will learn the prayers that go before and after it as well, but for now you should at least start reading the *Shema* every day.

JL: And what is it supposed to do?

AA: It is the *Shema*, we read it every morning and evening.

JL: Yes, but what's the purpose?

AA: It is a *mitzvah*, something commanded in the Torah. We do it because we are commanded to do it. There are many *mitzvot* that we do for no other reason than that they are commanded in the Torah. In this case there is another answer to your question, but I must be sure that you have understood what I said before: Judaism is about serving God. It is not about producing effects on oneself, it is not self-improvement, nor self-anything for that matter. You must be clear on this from the start.

JL: Okay.

AA: The other answer to your question is this: our Rabbis identified a different theme in each of the three paragraphs. The first they called "acceptance of God's kingship," because in saying these words, "*Shema Yisrael . . .*" and the rest, we set our hearts to accepting, to renewing in our hearts, God's sovereignty over all the things of this world. The second paragraph speaks specifically of the *mitzvot*, and so in saying it we set our hearts to taking on the duty of the *mitzvot* this day and every day, for they are what give expression to our awareness of God's sovereignty. And so, by the way, the order of which we spoke before, doing first and then understanding, is here reversed. And to my mind it is a good thing, for if in practice doing functions as a way of opening a place for understanding, nevertheless God's sovereignty, and our affirmation of it, should logically precede and be independent of anything that we may actually undertake to *do*.

JL: And what is the third part?

AA: The third paragraph concludes with mention of our going out of Egypt long ago, and for this reason (though most of the paragraph is concerned with other matters) it is sometimes called "the exodus from Egypt," because in saying it we thus call to mind the fact of that exodus.

JL: Is it because the exodus has some sort of symbolic meaning for us today?

AA: Look, Judd. You will not get far at that rate.

JL: What?

AA: This is the *mitzvah*. All you have to do is to say it. Try not to figure it all out, and certainly not that way; just say it. In Hebrew of course—I should have mentioned that right away. Hebrew is really the key to the whole thing.

Hebrew

JL: Now why is Hebrew so important? I'm afraid it's starting to look like this "crash course" is going to be a lifelong undertaking. Of course, I can understand that translations are not always clear, anybody who's studied literature knows that. But learning a new language is a lot more than I was bargaining for, especially one like Hebrew. You can't mean that it's impossible to pray to God, or even to understand the Torah, in English. . . .

AA: That isn't what I said. In fact it was specifically established that the *Shema* and prayers—and other things as well—could be said in any language. But it is certainly better to learn Hebrew and to begin to say all these things in the original. And what is the difficulty? A person who is studying in a graduate school ought not to be frightened by a new language, least of all by Hebrew.

JL: Why "least of all"? To begin with, there's a whole new alphabet to be learned.

AA: To learn the alphabet takes an adult an evening or an afternoon, no more. Then, with a little practice, you will be perfectly at home in it. As for the language itself, it all depends how far you want to go. If you wish only to be able to understand the words of the prayers and the Torah, you ought to be able to acquire the basic grammar and vocabulary in as little as a month or two, if you work steadily. I don't mean that you will never have to look up a word thereafter, but with a basic vocabulary you will be able to follow an extraordinary amount. And nowadays it is so easy to get to such a point. There are Hebrew courses in universities, in synagogues, and so forth, or—given what I am coming to recognize as your aversion to such settings—there are any number of do-it-yourself textbooks and tape recordings (though the latter generally aim at equipping you to order pastries in a Tel Aviv café). For that matter, you can go to Israel for a few months and follow a "crash course" there; that is probably the most efficient.

JL: Maybe so, but I'm still back at the theoretical issue. Why Hebrew? Certainly there are dozens, maybe hundreds, of different translations and commentaries on the Torah in English. No matter how well the average person learns Hebrew I can't imagine that he or she can achieve any greater insight into the text than these translators and commentators already have. The same is true of translations of the prayerbook. Unless, despite what you said, you're suggesting that a person has to pray in Hebrew.

AA: Not at all. As I mentioned, prayers can be said in any language. In fact, our prayerbook contains some that were written in Aramaic, a language that eventually replaced Hebrew in the daily speech of Jews both in ancient Israel and outside of it. But still, to my mind at least, there are some important, perhaps crucial, advantages to be gained by your learning at least enough Hebrew to be able to say and understand the prayers, as well as to read the Torah and our other books.

JL: What advantages?

AA: First of all, Hebrew gives you access to the synagogue service in a way that you would not otherwise have. Right now I'm sure that your memory of being in the synagogue is largely one of frustration and confusion, trying to "find the place" or keep up with the reader. This of course empties the synagogue of its purpose. As a child, no doubt you encountered many things in life that were frustrating or confusing, so the synagogue was hardly unique in this respect. But now, as an adult, you are in a position to act on your own, and there is no reason to continue treating yourself as a child. A little serious and concentrated effort on your part will utterly transform this part of Jewish life. Beyond this, of course, is the matter of translations that you mentioned: for so long as you don't know *something* of the language, you will always read such translations as if blind. However, once you have some feeling for how Hebrew works—even if you still depend on translations to a large extent—you will be able to make sense of what the translator is doing or to compare one translation with another intelligently. What is more, since much of later Jewish writings (the Talmud, and other books you may have heard of) is of an interpretive character—that is, devoted to explaining the precise meaning of this or that phrase in the Bible or another text—you will not really be equipped to understand the argument of these later books even in translation unless you can understand a little of the biblical Hebrew that they are seeking to explain. Again, you needn't become a master of the language. But a little learning will take you a long way.

Beyond all of these, however, is a rather more sublime point, and it was the "crucial" advantage of which I spoke. For the fact is that a language is much more than a mere vehicle for thoughts; it shapes thoughts. Anyone who knows more than one language well, truly well, can tell you this. If, as was my case, a person grows up speaking French and then at some later point moves to an English-speaking environment, he will learn the new language and soon reach the point that we call fluency, that is, he speaks the language without hesitation and without having to search for his words. But he does not yet speak English like a native. (Here I am not talking about his accent or pronunciation, which may never be perfect—but this is quite irrelevant to my point.) Although he "thinks in English," that is, he does not consciously translate from his native tongue, the thoughts that he formulates in English are still French thoughts, effortlessly rendered into English via a series of word equivalences that have long since become automatic; but the formulations themselves and, more than this, the ideas behind them, are still not really English. Then, by dint of living here, his *thinking* actually begins to change. The process takes five years, with some people ten years, or even longer; but eventually the way he chooses to approach a certain subject or make a certain observation, indeed, the very things that it occurs to him to say, will become English and not French. I do not know if professional linguists have a name for this phenomenon, but

I know it to be true from my own life and from my family's. And this is a profound change. For then, when he goes to speak his native language – even if he has continued to speak that language at home in his new country – the English thoughts will intrude in his native speech. Just as before, French thoughts were being effortlessly rendered in English, now English thoughts will find expression, sometimes even awkward expression, in the language of which he used to be a native master.

JL: I'm not sure I see the connection with Hebrew.

AA: It is simply that, to put it as an apparent truism, Hebrew is the language in which Hebrew thoughts occur. To pray in Hebrew, to read the Torah in Hebrew, is to give to yourself the language in which certain thoughts and ideas are at home.

JL: And why is that so important?

AA: Because those thoughts and ideas are the fabric of Judaism. For Hebrew, as I said, is the language of the Torah and of our other writings, the language in which God has the names we spoke of (and not "Lord"), the language in which He speaks to Moses and other human beings, and in which He has mercy and forgives and remembers. That language constitutes a world, a sphere of action, and not a closed one: you too may enter it by learning the language and reading and remembering the texts. And then, with the language inside of you – well, it is just as with the *mitzvot,* the "doing" part of Judaism: it opens up a space inside. So here, Hebrew too opens up a space inside you and allows these words to come back to you. Like the English thoughts that begin to intrude on the French native speaker, so Hebrew thoughts now have an opportunity to intrude on your own thinking and allow you to see what otherwise you might be blind to. This is one reason, by the way, that Hebrew is called *leshon ha-kodesh,* "the holy language." It is not that one language is intrinsically, by its origin or structure, holier than another. But Hebrew, by dint of being the language of Torah, ultimately became the location, the world, of a certain way of seeing.

The Advantage of a Poet

AA: Well, I suppose that our course could continue, but I think that, with this bit of orientation, you will have a number of specific things to pursue. If you wish it, we can talk again. But what you have to do now you must do on your own, back home.

JL: There is one thing that you still haven't told me that I am curious about, the advantage that writing poetry has for understanding Judaism. Is it only what you mentioned before, the thing about details?

AA: No, there is another. But rather than discuss it right away, I would prefer it if first you would tell me something about the business of being a poet. You know, no one who grows up in the Middle East can be insensitive to poetry, and I confess that in my youth I too wrote poems. Still, I was just an amateur, whereas you – your father has shown me poems of yours in literary magazines and even the popular monthlies, and I can see that you are no amateur. So tell me, what is it like for you to write a poem? Does it all come to you in a flash or do you do it bit by bit? And is there such a thing as inspiration?

JL: Many people ask about that, but I think the answer is different for different writers. For me, I can say this, that the job of being a poet consists mostly of devoting the time. You have to say, "I am going to put aside the time, my best time, so that I will be ready."

AA: Ready for what?

JL: I mean that some days you sit down to write something and nothing works. It's just– blank. But then there are other times when it seems to come out of nowhere—I don't mean to speak in terms of inspiration (to answer your other question), it might just as easily have to do with vitamins or phases of the moon; but there's no doubt that there are times when it just comes. And the point is that you have no way of knowing in advance, so you just have to be ready.

AA: And tell me something else. How do you decide *what* you are going to write about?

JL: Again, different people work in different ways. But for me, I have rarely sat down and said, "I'm going to write about such-and-such." Usually I just try to work it out of the words themselves—I start with something, an image or a phrase or something, and try to see where it leads. And of course what I write will always end up having to do in some way with whatever's on my mind or what's happened to me lately, but usually I don't start out trying to deal with those things directly. Actually, my ideas about this probably sound a little old-fashioned nowadays, since some poets in America just now seem to be championing a very deliberate, even manipulative, sort of writing, whereas I'm still very much stuck in that old way of thinking that holds that the best part of poetry is that which does not answer to any purely conscious intention on the poet's part. One arranges the circumstances and little more. This is the thing that ultimately makes poetry so difficult and, if I may say so, in its own way so spiritual. For in the end poems are not made *out* of anything at all, no raw material except the very words that everybody uses to think and speak with; and whatever a poem ends up talking about, its words themselves will have been fought for, wrestled out of a great silence and an utterly blank piece of paper. This sometimes seems to me so elemental, the poet sitting there in that moment trying to make something in the silence and give it shape. Because of course the moment, the silence, always threaten simply to remain impenetrable and not give up anything. And what is particularly difficult about the thing that he's trying to do is that he must not just to come up with *something,* and not even just with something that sounds good. Of course, what we prize in poems is that they take wonderful advantage of the language, that they sound good—but that's only half of it. The other half, the half that's in fact often in conflict with the first, is that they also have to try to be true, they have to touch on something that's important and to try to tell the truth about it and not just to make something that sounds impressive or clever or musical or whatever. Sometimes the truth is not the elegant or clever thing you could have said; sometimes the truth sounds lousy. And so a poet is always somehow engaged in this struggle, in which, as I said, he really doesn't have any weapons at all, nothing except his own honesty in just trying to be there in that particular moment and make something out of it, using the words that everybody uses but trying to make something that will be good and true.

AA: You have put it very well. But can you guess from your own answer why it was that I asked the question I did?

JL: Perhaps.

AA: You see, there is much in common between your answer and what I was trying in my own way to say. Of course, writing poetry is an activity quite apart. And yet this struggle-without-weapons that you describe must sound familar to anyone who is truly a Jew. Because in the end the person who goes out to stand before God goes out in just that fashion: everything is peeled away, and he has only his small self and the very particular situation of his being, at that particular moment, here on earth seeking to face God.

JL: I see what you mean.

AA: Yet you don't sound very enthusiastic about it.

JL: You see, I was hoping it would be very different and not more of the same. I don't need more of the same.

AA: Oh it is, it is quite different, but not in a way that you might imagine now. The comparison is really, well, not superficial, but misleading in this respect. Because in the end Judaism is, as I said, about the service of God, and this is light-years away from making poems.

It is only the starting position that is the same, nothing more, but this is nonetheless something. For all the rest that Judaism is must be built upon that quiet, honest, stripped-down state, the state of the one who goes out without weapons. And this is the advantage of a poet, that he will have been there before.

PART III

The time: some months later

Books

JL: I'm not sure things have really been going that well since we talked, although I did try some of what you suggested. I've been sitting in on Gruber's course, "Introduction to Judaism," and I went to services a couple of times at the university.

AA: Yes?

JL: But it wasn't really what I was expecting; it's not exactly what you said.

AA: No?

JL: No. In fact, I get the feeling that everybody there is talking *around* the main point. I mean, at least when you and I talked last time, it seemed that we were more or less on the same wavelength, that we both were talking about the same goal. All right, you warned me about synagogues, so I did not expect too much from that. But "Introduction to Judaism" is really just about what the different holidays are, and Jewish history, and Jewish books—Torah, Mishnah, Talmud, midrash, etc., etc.

AA: What is wrong with that?

JL: Nothing's wrong with it, it just seems, you know, somewhat beside the point. In fact, most of the time I feel like saying, Come on, come clean—this isn't what it's really about, is it? I mean, I don't mind learning facts and the names of things and so forth, I do that all the time anyway. . . . But it does seem basically irrelevant to what we were talking about.

AA: But Judd, you are just beginning. Really, what have you accomplished? I told you, Judaism is a whole world, and you are barely beginning to open your eyes to see it. I know what we said last time, but you are just beginning. You must plunge yourself into every aspect of Judaism, everything. And as I explained, given the state of affairs in America, you must take help from wherever you can get it—synagogues and courses and books and whatever. You've learned how to be an American for more than twenty years, but you are just starting to learn to be a Jew. It is not a small thing.

JL: Yes, but what I'm saying is that I don't really see the point. Okay, learning Hebrew we talked about, and I can see some purpose to that, and even learning prayers by heart. But all the other things—what's a commentary on what, what was written when—I just don't see how it all fits in.

AA: The point is that you know nothing. This is painful for anyone to admit, but especially so for someone in your position. And so you focus on what it is that you imagine you want to learn and then try to push aside the rest. This will not work. Or I suppose it will work, in an American sort of way, in the hobbylike thing that Judaism has become for so many of your compatriots—learn a song or two, take a course in Jewish mysticism, and there you are. But as I said, Judaism is not a hobby, it is a way of living. And that way of living consists, as I said, of details; everything emerges from the blessed details. So you have to begin from the beginning and learn and learn—absorb whatever you can, really, since there is no set order in which things are to be learned, and you will in any case come back again and again to the same things in different contexts until they are familiar. Do you understand?

JL: Yes, but I can't say that this is very encouraging. You mean I have to spend the next twenty years catching up to where I should be now?

AA: I did not say that. How fast you go depends on you. But do not be so soft on yourself. If you work hard, in six months or a year you will be well on your way. The point is that you must resist trying to get away with a little, resist letting your fear scale down the job to something small. Because being a Jew is not a hobby, reserved for weekends or an hour or two in the evening. Do you understand?

JL: I understand what you're saying, yes.

AA: Judd, if you want to stop, we can stop here.

JL: No.

AA: Good. Now let us see what you have learned so far. You have been studying about books?

JL: What the books themselves are isn't much of a problem. But as a matter of fact, one thing that hasn't been very clear in the course is the relationship between them—Torah, Mishnah, and so forth. There's a definite hierarchy, isn't there?

AA: In a sense, yes. In any case, the matter is straightforward. We have first of all the Torah, that is, the first five books of the Bible, called in English Genesis, Exodus, Leviticus, Numbers, and Deuteronomy. (In Hebrew they are each known by the first or key word in their opening sentences, thus *Bereshit, Shemot, Vayyikra, Bemidbar,* and *Devarim.*) These books are sometimes called the Five Books of Moses, because they come from Moses and because the latter four of them are framed by the story of his life. (The first book, *Bereshit,* is about the earliest history of our people, from before the time of Abraham, our first father, and on to the history of Abraham's son and grandson, Isaac and Jacob, and the twelve sons of Jacob whose descendants ultimately made up the twelve tribes of the people of Israel.) Added to these first five books are the other books of the Bible. Some, like Joshua and Judges and Samuel and Kings and so forth, are basically history. They tell the story of what happened from the time of Moses' death onward—our early settlement in the land of Israel, the rise of David and the establishment of his royal dynasty, how the kingdom he established eventually split into two, and so forth down to the time in the sixth century B.C.E. when the Babylonians conquered Jerusalem and destroyed the Temple and exiled the Jewish people to Babylon. In fact, the history continues after that, in books like Ezra and Nehemiah, which describe how the Jews then

67

returned to their land seventy years later, after the Babylonians were overthrown, and how they rebuilt the Temple. Besides these books of history are books of prophecy like Isaiah and Jeremiah, Hosea and Amos and the others, that contain the words and accounts of prophets who came long after the time of Moses and spoke to the people on behalf of God. And in addition to these are yet other books, the Psalms of David, the sayings of Solomon, the book of Job, and several more. All of them have been preserved from ancient times with the greatest care and treated with special sanctity.

JL: But what makes the time of Moses so special? I mean, why should the first five books be *the* Torah and the rest just be something else?

AA: Actually, although we use *Torah* to refer to the first five books, the ancient Rabbis sometimes used this term to speak of the entire Bible; in fact, all of classical Jewish learning was Torah, that is, "sacred learning," to them. But in any case, it is not the *history* found in the first five books that gives them their special importance, but the *mitzvot,* the divine commandments, that set out the basics of the Jewish way of life: how to worship God, the necessity of keeping the Sabbath and holidays and so forth, and how to act in everyday life. You see, in the course of narrating the events of the people during the time of Moses, the text also tells of the various commandments that were given at that time by God to the Jewish people, centering, of course, on the great revelation at Mount Sinai. These commandments are the foundation of Judaism. They provide the basic blueprint for leading our lives as closely as possible in keeping with God's will. And so in this sense they, the *mitzvot,* are really the heart of the Torah – and one reason why it, more than any other part of the Bible, is at the very center of Jewish life. Tradition holds that there are in fact 613 different commandments to be found in the Torah, and these form the basis of our whole *halakhah.*

JL: Are there no commandments in the Bible outside of the Torah?

AA: None. Or more precisely, the other books have a somewhat different status with regard to commandments. All the books that I have mentioned were written down and kept because they too were held to be sacred, and we study them all and heed their admonitions. But as regards the 613 *mitzvot,* these other books are important only to the extent that they illuminate many of the things touched on in the Torah. And of course in this respect they are sometimes crucial— so that our Rabbis held, for example, that the whole people of Israel, including the generations yet to be born, were all present in spirit at Mount Sinai when the Torah was given, and that whatever later prophets uttered they thus uttered because they too had been present at Sinai. By saying this they meant to stress that there is but one divine teaching, the Torah, and it is reflected in the rest of the Bible as in the words of later sages and rabbis. But as for the *mitzvot* themselves, they are all located within the Torah.

JL: So then is or is not the rest of the Bible considered subordinate to the first five books?

AA: From the standpoint of the *mitzvot,* yes. But it might be more to the point to say simply that the Torah came first: it was given to us through Moses at Mount Sinai, and since then it has been our sacred guide. But history did not end there, nor did instruction—as I said, there were prophets and teachers who all taught further and explained, and their words have been preserved as well.

JL: By the way, is "Bible" a Christian term? And what about "Old Testament"?

AA: This is a difficult bit of terminology. Our English word "Bible" entered the language, understandably, via Christianity; but the word ultimately goes back to the Greek *ta biblía,* "the books." Apparently Greek-speaking Jews, and later Christians as well, used to refer to the Bible as simply "*the* books," or "the sacred books." In English, therefore, "Bible" is a perfectly acceptable term for Jews to use. On the other hand, "Old Testament" is clearly a Christian term and should be avoided. For our sacred texts only began to be called the "Old" Testament (or "old covenant," for this is the true meaning of the term) by Christians because of the Christian doctrine of a "New" Testament or covenant.

JL: How do they say "Bible" in Hebrew?

AA: There isn't one special term. Our classical texts sometimes use the word *ha-katuv*, which means "that which is written," "Scripture," and sometimes *mikra*, "that which is read." A very frequent expression is *kitvei ha-kodesh*, "the sacred writings." And *Torah*, although it is generally used to refer to the first five books, is sometimes used in a more inclusive sense as well. There are still other terms and forms of reference in rabbinic texts. But nowadays people in Israel generally say *miqra* or else *tanakh*, the latter being an acronym for *torah, nevi'im,* and *ketuvim*, the three main divisions of the text, that is, Torah, the Prophets, and the other Writings.

JL: And what about the other books I mentioned, the Mishnah and so forth—what are they, and what is their relationship to the books in the Bible?

AA: From the time the Torah was given, its words alone were not in themselves a complete guide to the fulfillment of the *mitzvot*. You can see this yourself with regard to Shabbat or any of the other sorts of things that make up our daily existence. While the Torah provides the framework, exactly what we are to do and to avoid doing, and how and in what manner, all needs to be filled in. Beyond this, there are some aspects of our everyday affairs that the Torah hardly treats at all. One could hardly think of more common legal concerns in daily life than, for example, marriage and divorce, landlord-tenant laws, business relations—yet these and dozens of other topics are only hinted at in the Torah, so here too some filling in of the details was necessary. For centuries this filling in was passed along orally, from the time of Moses onward, and in fact came to be called the *torah she-be'al peh*, the "oral Torah," as opposed to written Scripture, the *torah she-bikhtav*.

JL: Why wasn't it written down? In fact, why wasn't it part of the written Torah in the first place?

AA: Many answers are given for that. Perhaps it was that even at the beginning a single written Torah with all the details would have been far too cumbersome; perhaps it was that, in leaving the oral Torah unwritten, provision was made for its expansion so as to include later matters – the holiday of Purim, for example – that did not exist at the time of Moses; or perhaps it was that prescribing oral transmission for part of the Torah insured a certain kind of study that a written document alone might not guarantee (since an oral Torah requires two people, a teacher and a student, and sets a certain relationship between them). It may well be, as yet another of our traditions has it, that the oral Torah vouchsafed that only Israel would possess the whole of Torah, since an unwritten text cannot be translated and distributed to other nations (as did in fact soon happen with the written Bible). Whatever the reason, this is the origin of that other part of our sacred teachings, the things written down in the Mishnah and Talmud and the other texts you mentioned.

JL: So it did eventually get written down anyway.

AA: Yes, that's true. Starting at the end of the second century of the common era, conditions in Israel necessitated giving a fixed and established form to these teachings, and one result was the Mishnah. It probably was not "published" in book form right away, but it was set in fixed form and eventually did get copied, though for centuries its primary form of transmission continued to be oral, from teacher to student.

JL: But this is the part that's never really clear. We're supposed to have a Bible, but then we also have the Mishnah, and I suppose the Talmud too, which on the one hand are clearly *not* part of the Bible, and on the other hand are supposed to be *like* it, or even part of it, at least in terms of their importance and authoritativeness.

AA: I suppose your difficulty arises in part from your upbringing. Because of course Christianity never did have the oral Torah, and so, since it has only "the Bible," you, brought up in a Christian country, think this is the natural state of affairs. But it isn't necessarily. These two bodies of books, one originally oral, the other written, are complementary and together make up the basic texts of Judaism. If names like Mishnah and midrash are unfamiliar to you, well, I trust that will change soon.

JL: Who wrote these other books?

AA: As I said, the process of transmitting the oral Torah is held to have started with Moses himself. But the putting of it in definitive form owes much to a particular group of teachers who lived just at the beginning of the common era, from the first century on. This was a crucial time for Judaism, a time when various sects and claims were forcing clear definitions and positions, so that the activities of these teachers played a very important role. They were also the first to bear the title *rabbi,* which means literally "my teacher" or "my master," and so today we sometimes speak of them simply as "the Rabbis" or, in Hebrew, *ḥazal,* an acronym for "our sages of blessed memory." You may learn some of their names if you have not yet already: Hillel and Shammai, Yoḥanan ben Zakkai, Rabban Gamliel, Rabbi Akiva, and many others.

JL: So you might say that Judaism is really as much the religion of the Rabbis as it is of Moses.

AA: Judaism is the religion of the Jewish people. In some respects it began even before Sinai, with our earliest ancestors, and it has, of course, been passed on from generation to generation since then. But the Rabbis crystallized many things and defined their form for the future.

JL: Now as to the books, I mean, other than the Bible itself—

AA: We have already mentioned the Mishnah, which, as I said, was passed on through the ages and put in its definitive form around 200 C.E. It is not terribly long—nowdays it can be printed in a single, medium-sized volume—and consists of six parts, corresponding to six major spheres of human activity: "Seeds," the first part, covers agricultural laws; "Sacred Time" covers Shabbat and the festivals; and so forth. Each part is divided into chapters, which list specific regulations connected with its topic. Although these topics are often related to particular *mitzvot* in the Torah—for the oral Torah, as I said, provides many of the practical details for properly carrying out the *mitzvot* and thus the substance of our *halakhah*—they only rarely refer

72

explicity to verses in the Torah. In some cases this is because there is relatively little to refer to; as the Talmud itself observes, while some parts of our *halakhah* are completely rooted in the written text of the Torah, other parts are, as they expressed it, like "mountains suspended by a hair," that is, enormously detailed provisions in the oral Torah that elaborate only the slightest passing reference in the written one; while still other parts, it says, "float in midair." Given this state of affairs, it would be impossible for the Mishnah to refer back to the text consistently and systematically. But there is another, still more practical, consideration.

JL: What is that?

AA: It has to do with the way the Mishnah was learned. As the name implies (*mishnah* comes from the Hebrew root meaning to "say twice" or "repeat"), the Mishnah was learned by heart, in order. In the olden days, a gifted scholar could simply rattle off the entire content of the book from beginning to end. Learned in this fashion, the Mishnah had of necessity to be relatively brief, imparting its information in topical order and without reference to the Torah. This was not the only form of study, however. People of course also studied the Bible, verse by verse, and when they studied in this fashion, explanations of each verse, including material such as that contained in the Mishnah, were presented as well. So this was another way in which the oral Torah, the *torah she-be'al peh,* was imparted. This method of study was called not *mishnah* but *midrash,* "interpretation," because the material was organized into interpretations of individual verses. Just as the one form of study yielded a book called Mishnah, so the other yielded a series of books called midrash. There is a collection of midrash, or verse-by-verse interpretations, not only for each book of the Torah, but for virtually every book of the Bible—in fact, in not a few cases there is more than one midrashic collection for the same book, as well as books of midrash arranged on some other principle. Perhaps it was in part because of their size and number that these books, despite their great popularity, never did attain the same central status or importance as the Mishnah.

JL: What about the Talmud?

AA: I have already said that Mishnah was learned by heart, taught by teacher to student. But this process involved not only memorizing the words, but also understanding their meaning and application, because the language is always clipped and sometimes purposely cryptic. After a while, especially with more advanced students, it apparently became customary not only to go over the significance of the particular words of the Mishnah being learned, but also to raise all manner of theoretical issues connected to them, to examine—just as one might nowadays in a law school seminar—all sides of the question being discussed and even go off on some well-planned tangents. These discussions, organized around each little section of the Mishnah, were ultimately written down and became the Talmud. In fact, there are two Talmuds, corresponding to the two great centers of Jewish learning in late antiquity, the Land of Israel and Babylon.

JL: Which is *the* Talmud?

AA: Both are studied, but the Babylonian Talmud was historically much more influential. For the Babylonian center ultimately became the dominant one, and our present traditions and learning (and, incidentally, our prayers as well) have come to us via this center. In fact, the Babylonian Talmud might be called the great compendium of Jewish learning outside of the Bible. It has everything—it presents, and then explains and interprets the Mishnah itself, bit by bit, and so provides the basis for our *halakhah*; but in so doing it endlessly refers back to the Torah (as the Mishnah itself did not) and often also to passages elsewhere in the Bible, so that, in effect, most of the whole Bible ends up being explicated too. And in addition to this, there are vignettes from the lives of the Rabbis, humorous or whimsical narratives, and much more. Nowadays printed editions of the Babylonian Talmud can run to twenty large volumes. I admit that most of this is not the text of the Talmud itself but various later commentaries on it—still, you could see how one might spend a lifetime just reading through it carefully.

JL: Great.

74

AA: Perhaps you can take comfort in knowing that virtually everyone who first contemplates the Jewish library feels overwhelmed. In fact, there is an expression in Hebrew, *yam shel talmud,* the "sea of learning," that well captures the sense of helplessness one first experiences before this enormous body of material. And I have not nearly finished the list. But you also may take comfort in this: although this sea is there, one need not try to get across it all at once or even survey its circumference.

JL: What do you mean?

AA: I mean, first of all, that what you need to know to live as a Jew, to follow the *halakhah* and to function fully within Judaism, you can learn fairly easily and, quite probably, without even turning directly to any of these books. You will learn what you need to know simply by being around people who do know it, by going to synagogue and to other people's houses—Jews you may know at the university—or, if you want, by consulting codes and guides to the practical observance of our *halakhah,* some of them even in English. But the "sea" of books I mentioned, and specifically the study of the Talmud or of the Bible with its traditional commentaries, has another function in Judaism. It is an activity in itself, plunging into our sacred texts and understanding their thinking, and this activity is in fact a *mitzvah,* a central part of the Jewish way. Sometimes, of course, the material studied does have some practical consequence for our daily lives, but often what we learn are things like the procedures that once existed in the Temple in Jerusalem, laws concerning sacrifices or ritual purification and the like; and this should highlight an important aspect of study in Judaism. Because for us it is *studying,* the activity itself, that counts, and not necessarily the practical application, and certainly not the quantity mastered.

Do not mistake me—one aims to learn much, to become saturated in Torah. But formulating it in the way I did, I meant my description to imply that the essence of study in Judaism is the act of immersing oneself in the world of these texts, dwelling in them for a few minutes or a few hours each day. Indeed, if the purpose were otherwise, surely the *mitzvah* would have been stated in some other fashion, specifying, for example, that one must learn such-and-such books thoroughly and then one will have fulfilled it, or that one must spend a certain amount of time each day. Instead, study is one of the few *mitzvot* which, as our Rabbis said, *ein lahem shi'ur*—they have no limit, there is no amount that you can do and be said to have done enough. This means that even if you were to devote yourself exclusively to studying the Talmud for the rest of your life and managed to get through it all before you died (which only a relatively few can manage), you would then still have to go on to some other text or commentary or else go back to the beginning and start all over again. Because returning to these texts, spending time with them—as much as possible—is what counts.

JL: But why this whole emphasis on study?

AA: Again, there are many answers. Obviously, there is a relationship between study and the carrying out of our *halakhah*. The whole strength of our way, as I have said, lies in the "blessed details," and these require regular attention, so that our slightest actions before God can be precise and deliberate, and performed with understanding. And so one studies in order to better live in keeping with the Torah and to perform the *mitzvot* properly, and in studying one inevitably learns in general to treat *mitzvot* with greater care and to follow the example of the Rabbis, who were so exact in their actions and zealous for the *halakhah* in all its particulars.

Second of all, the thing about study (or *talmud Torah*, as we call it) is that it is a *mitzvah* that is always at hand, so to speak. Just because there is no fixed time to undertake it, it is something that one can take up whenever a spare minute is available—or, indeed, that one can take on as a lifetime career. And, as you will see, it is a combination of pleasures—a pleasure to turn one's heart to Torah, first of all, and an intellectual pleasure in figuring things out, following the logic or anticipating the questions. What is more, since study is best undertaken with a friend or in a group, there is also the pleasure of fellowship and collaboration.

But there is yet another reason for the importance of study in Judaism, and one connected to things we have seen before. For by now

76

you know that the world in which one lives is not of indifferent importance to how one ends up thinking and understanding. The language one speaks, the things one talks about with one's friends and neighbors, at work and in stores and at home, the petty concerns of the day—all these end up doing much more than just filling our day: they compose a world, an understanding of reality, nothing less. For they are constantly interpreting things for us, setting priorities, putting ideas before us, words in our minds; they inculcate and reinforce the common view of the world, every minute of the day. And we take it all in, whether we want to or not. Nor certainly has it escaped you that there is a great disparity between this modernday understanding of the world and that found elsewhere—and especially the understanding presumed and elaborated in Judaism. And so for us, to study these texts is to enter a different world, the world of Torah. To enter that world is to perceive and understand our own world in a different way. I might say that study is, in the best sense, a subversive activity, since it helps to relax the stranglehold that our daily existence has on our perceptions and allows us to glimpse the world as if from another perspective.

JL: I see. But what was the reason for the emphasis on study in olden times? I mean before there was this dissonance.

AA: I don't know what you mean by "olden times." For certainly this aspect of study was well known even to our ancient Rabbis. In a famous parable, Rabbi Akiva, who lived in the second century, compared the world of the Torah to the sea and ourselves to fish within it, whom (he said) Roman culture sought to lure onto the dry land. In other words, immersion in the study of Torah was even then understood to constitute an environment wholly different from the everyday world of Roman-occupied Judea. And so I believe it is today. Of course, all of us nowadays have some contact with the "dry land"—in that sense we may be more like amphibians than fish—and perhaps this was even the case long ago. Our Rabbis, in fact, had a phrase to designate the proper path, *Torah im derekh eretz,* "Torah along with the everyday world." And this is precisely why our *halakhah* is what it is: we are to live in the world and go about our daily occupations, but one day a week we put aside all our regular preoccupations because it is Shabbat, and even during the workday week, three times a day we stop what we are doing to say the fixed words of prayer, and stop to say the *Shema* morning and evening, and so on with the other things. It is the same also with study, except that here we not only put aside one world but actively enter another. Indeed, this is yet another sense in which Torah is, as we have seen, like water.

JL: What do you mean?

AA: Well it is not only, as Rabbi Akiva implied, that Torah is an environment, a habitat, and not only that, as water does for all creatures, so Torah sustains our lives, and yet is easily available to all, and can in fact be had for free. In all these ways, our Rabbis taught, is Torah like water. But what is more, like water, Torah also purifies and cleanses. Thus, we go about our way in the world and do what is necessary for our existence, but when we can, we turn aside and enter the world of Torah. It does not matter what you happen to be studying, whether Mishnah or Talmud or the Bible with its commentaries; that world, the Hebrew words, the issues of *halakhah* and of interpretation, the characteristic way the Rabbis have of trying to make sense of the biblical text—all these make taking up one of these books less like studying in the sense that you know it than like joining a familiar company for an hour or two and seeing well-known faces in a slightly different setting or in the process of exploring some new piece of territory. Now this form of study, despite the pleasure one comes to feel in doing it, is no mere diversion. As I suggested, it is really a way of entering a different understanding of the world, in which different things are important; and even upon leaving it and returning to the humdrum world, we for a while take some of it with us, and everyday life is changed for it. And so, as the comparison to water suggests, immersion in Torah is like immersion in a purifying brook or stream, from which one emerges both refreshed and clean.

Music

_JL:_ What you're saying is that studying in Judaism isn't mainly a matter of learning certain specific things —

_AA:_ It is and it is not. But beyond that, it is part of the way we turn our lives to God.

_JL:_ I can understand that. Although you'll have to admit, it seems a little roundabout.

_AA:_ What do you mean?

_JL:_ It's what I was saying before: everything in Judaism seems sort of indirect. I mean, wouldn't it be much more to the point to say to people, okay, now spend the next two hours meditating, or praying or whatever? Even if studying is, as you say, a means of purifying, it seems a strange way to get to that end.

_AA:_ What I was saying about purification was not really a description of the _purpose_ of study in Judaism, but, as it were, a side effect. The purpose of study, the reason why we do it, is simply because it is a _mitzvah_. We try every day to carry out what was commanded us in the Torah itself.

_JL:_ Yes, but if there's a more concentrated or direct way of achieving the same thing. . . .

_AA:_ What "same thing"? Judd, I fear you still have not shaken the "jogging" mentality. I told you before: Judaism is not about producing results, it is about serving God. In this sense your whole orientation is wrong. If you wish to feel better or more refreshed, then I suggest that you look into something else.

JL: But I don't understand. Weren't you just talking about leaving off your daily occupations for an hour or two to study, then coming back again? You can call the one jogging and the other the service of God, but I don't really see the difference.

AA: The difference could not be clearer. Our purpose is to turn our lives to God. And so if we had been commanded to spend our days (as it were) playing the piano or juggling rubber balls, then that is what we would do. The same of course would be true if the Torah had told us to sit and contemplate the mountains for fourteen hours a day: we would do it. But of course the very essence of Judaism is quite the opposite: what was revealed to us at Sinai directed us instead to turn our *everyday lives,* in their full everydayness, to God's service, demanding not only that we seek to be mindful of God in the midst of our regular activities, but that we shape our day-to-day relations with neighbors in consequence, or relations between parents and children, and so forth. It is with just such things that the laws given at Sinai are concerned. Because these daily activities are to be the instruments, the raw material. Do you see?

JL: Yes. I suppose.

AA: Perhaps you already know a certain feeling you may get from time to time, a slowness or estrangement of sorts—as if you were suddenly intensely aware of nothing other than being where you happen to be. This is the feeling of the everydayness, here and now. Sometimes, when you are looking out the window or simply sitting in a sunny room, such a feeling may come over you. If so, then you will know why it is in the everyday, the down-to-earth, that Judaism is rooted. This is ground-zero, the beginning. Do not go looking for effects, Judd.

JL: What does it feel like?

AA: It does not matter. The point is, Judaism is not a way of escaping the everyday, or even transforming it, but living right in the midst of it.

80

JL: That may be true for you, but what about the ultra-Orthodox Jews you see, you know, the ones with the black coats and long beards and so forth—you could hardly describe them as plunged in the everyday! Don't they spend all their time contemplating the Torah?

AA: If you mean to refer to Jews like the Hasidim in Brooklyn and elsewhere, the truth is that they conform utterly to what I have been saying. In fact, they are a perfect example of how Judaism is about everyday life: they work, most of them, at regular jobs, in their neighborhoods or in Manhattan—some of them, by tradition, pursuing a particular trade, like diamond cutting, though others have now taken up such new specialties as computer programming—and in so doing their purpose is simply to lead fully Jewish lives, to go about their daily affairs completely as Jews. Of course, in every generation there are Jews who, by one circumstance or another, are enabled to make the study of Torah their full-time daily occupation—yet this is hardly the norm. When you study the Talmud you will see that even in ancient times Judaism was the religion of shoemakers and beer brewers and day laborers, dyers and cloth merchants. In this respect the Hasidim are perfectly representative of what I was saying. As for their black coats—well, this is another matter, it is simply their tradition.

JL: But isn't that how most Orthodox Jews dress?

AA: Oh no. The Hasidim are merely one community (or, rather, several different ones) that have transferred themselves to America and, in the process, have tried to remain faithful to everything that existed in their communities in the Old Country, whatever its original purpose or status. But there is no place in our writings where it says that you have to wear one of those broad-brimmed hats or black coats in order to be a faithful Jew! Indeed, it has often occurred to me that the profusion of "styles" of Judaism in America is a reflection of the fact that American Jews still have not found their own particular way of being Jewish.

JL: Is there more than one way to be Jewish—I mean, and still follow the *halakhah?*

AA: Oh yes, if you look around the world a bit, or only New York — look at the Iranian Jews who are here or the Baghdadis, Polish Hasidim, or the German Jews of upper Manhattan — you could hardly find a more heterogeneous-looking group of people than these. Of course, it is true that Jews all over the world share basically the same beliefs and practices: we all read from the same Torah each Shabbat, we say the same prayers (though here there are a few minor differences) and observe the same commandments. More even than these, we are, as I said before, one great family, with a single history and many lines interconnecting each community with the others, great and small. All Jews recognize this and feel it. Yet, as to how one goes about being a Jew, there is no small variety from place to place. And I must say that there was something unmistakably different about being a Jew in Aleppo — it's so palpable a difference that it sometimes seems to me a pity that there is no one external thing that one might point to and say, the difference comes from this!

JL: What do you think the cause might be?

AA: Ohh. . . . Here, my friend, you ask too much of me. Certainly it has something to do with the whole atmosphere, the mental world, in which one's being a Jew takes place. The mental world of the Jews themselves, to be sure, and perhaps that of the non-Jews also. I don't wish to idealize things, by the way. Life for the Jews of Aleppo was sometimes brutal, especially, in my life, starting in 1947. Besides that, of course, things were quite primitive by American standards, though probably not quite so backward as you would tend to imagine. But on this question of atmosphere, as I say, life was not at all as it is here. And — I think as a result — our style of being a Jew was very different.

JL: In what way?

AA: In all ways — how we thought of ourselves, first of all, but also what it meant for us to keep our festivals and our traditions, what the Sabbath was like, certain expressions we had, what it meant to go to the synagogue and the way things were done there, the leaders of our community, and on and on. Really, when I think about it I would have to say that not only were the details of what we did and how we did things sometimes different, but even two identical actions would have very different significances there and here, because of the different contexts, and as a consequence would have a different feel or flavor as well.

JL: I see.

AA: But in general about this question of different Jewish communities, it has often occurred to me that the situation is somewhat similar to that of a musician performing a piece of music. For musicians are quite bound by the composer's orders—they may not change a single note, nor even skip one, nor (generally speaking) alter the time or the key of the piece. What is more, the composer has even inserted little instructions along the way that say things like, "briskly, but not too fast," "with great tenderness," and so forth. One would think that, with so much pinned down and specified, one performance of the piece would be virtually identical with the next. Yet any music lover will tell you that it is quite otherwise, and that the greatest variations can be introduced by what a particular musician brings to the act of playing—not only his own individual talents, but his way of apprehending the composer's instructions. It is the same, it seems to me, with different Jewish communities around the world. We all have the same Torah, the same Mishnah, Talmud, basically even the same codifications of Jewish law, interpretations and decrees of later authorities; and of course we keep the same Sabbaths, festivals, and holy days. Yet in each place Jews come to these things with a slightly different spirit, a different way of seeing things—and, just as with the musicians, this can make for very large differences in what comes out.

JL: And what do you think of American Judaism's "music"?

AA: Only that it is still trying to find itself. And I am not at all sure that it will succeed.

JL: What do you mean?

AA: As you know, most American Jews are relatively recent arrivals on these shores: the vast majority immigrated only at the very end of the last century and the beginning of this one. Their Judaism—I mean their way of being Jews—is thus still fresh from the Old World. Now, most of these Jews came from eastern Europe, from Poland or Russia or Lithuania. Judaism there was a vibrant, wonderful thing—the Jews even had their own language, Yiddish, and a way of life that was steeped in all things Jewish. It was a glorious civilization, but one that, alas, cannot really be expected to continue in its old form in America. For in eastern Europe the Jews lived for the most part in tightly knit communities, often in little towns that were seventy or ninety or even one hundred percent Jewish. Children were sent to Jewish schools, where religious instruction was *the* curriculum— everyone learned Hebrew, everyone was versed in Torah at least to some extent, and, on the other hand, it was not uncommon for grown men to have virtually no knowledge of, say, elementary mathematics or geography or other aspects of secular culture, because these were judged to be simply irrelevant. (In the decades before World War II, some of this orientation had begun to change—but that is of no consequence for American Judaism.) Their world there was thus almost totally Jewish. Among themselves they spoke, as I said, in their own language, and that in itself should be a measure of their insularity. Here in America it is all quite different—the pattern of settlement, of course, and the degree of integration into the wider society, and the "Jewishness" of the Jews, not to speak of the great differences introduced by an infinitely higher standard of living, secular learning, technological changes, and so on and so on. To expect American Jews to continue being Jewish in the same way as their eastern European ancestors is, to return to the matter you mentioned, precisely like expecting them to continue wearing the same heavy black coats and fur hats that their ancestors wore in Poland.

JL: But that's just the point—don't they still wear precisely those things?

AA: Well, let me tell you. Those coats and fur hats were in fact once the mark of the Polish nobleman or bourgeois—that is, these items were hardly Jewish at their origin, but, if anything, Gentile. The Polish Jews adopted them because, back in the eighteenth century, when the Hasidic sects were being founded, this was simply what the smart

84

set wore. They merely wished to dress in the fashion of their day. But even after the styles then changed, the members of the sects I mentioned continued to wear this distinctive garb—not because it was "smart" any more, but because this was now the way that their fathers and grandfathers had dressed, and they were reluctant to change.

JL: I didn't know that.

AA: Oh yes. In fact, it is in general true that many of the things that people in this country, Jews and Gentiles alike, think of as Jewish are really only German or Polish or Russian in origin.

JL: Like what?

AA: Well, in concrete terms, such things as food: all those delicatessen items, for example, lox and bagels, herring in various sauces, kasha, and on and on—none of these is Jewish, only central or eastern European. And so it is with other Jewish dishes—perhaps all but that stomach-churning casserole the eastern European Jews are so fond of. . . . You know the kind I mean. . . .

JL: Kugel?

AA: Uggh. In any event, with that and perhaps a few other exceptions, most of what Americans think of as typically Jewish concoctions were really not Jewish at all—it is only that the Jews were the ones to bring them to this country, where they were unknown or at least uncommon, and so we associate them nowadays with their bearers and think of them as Jewish. So too, in more general terms, much of the more abstract way of being of those same Jews—their gestures, facial expressions, and more than that, even some habits of mind, what they notice, what they object to, how they present things, and so on and so forth—is not Jewish at all. I have known more than one New Yorker who has come back from a visit to Russia or Rumania with the verdict: "The people there seem so Jewish!" This should tell you something about what our notion of Jewish is based upon. And indeed, one has but to know Jews from elsewhere—from North Africa or the eastern Mediterranean—to know how superficial and local many of these supposedly universally Jewish traits are.

85

JL: Well, what is left? Is there nothing distinctively Jewish about Jews?

AA: Of course there is. To begin with, there are things uniquely Jewish that each community shares with the others: our *halakhah* and the way of life that it shapes, and, more even than that, the way it shapes our very thinking and view of the world. And we are, as I said before, genetically one family, and as a consequence we have many family resemblances. But besides these, there are many things which, whatever their origin, have been taken over by this or that Jewish community and become Jewish in the process. Yiddish is at bottom a dialect, or amalgam of dialects, of German. But when certain German-speaking Jews migrated eastward, they became separated thereby from their original linguistic environment, and their speech thus came to retain features that meanwhile had disappeared from other forms of German; and they themselves likewise transformed other aspects of their language, indeed, introduced many Hebrew words and expressions into their speech. The result was a new, and distinctly Jewish, language. So, similarly, is it with the black coats and hats we were discussing. These were originally Gentile dress, but the Jews, by retaining them even after fashions had changed, made them over into something characteristically their own.

JL: Then what makes you think they will ever change?

AA: Because there is nothing *essential* about them, just as there was nothing essential about Yiddish, despite even those Hebrew words. And so, in a different environment, such things usually do change or even disappear, however slowly or reluctantly. And you know, it is *hot* in those coats! In New York, or Tel Aviv for that matter, I am sure that it can get very uncomfortable wearing them in the summer, and even in the winter they can be a bit much now that there is central heating everywhere. . . . Perhaps they won't disappear all at once. But do you know that in Israel I have noticed that certain Hasidim now wear coats that only look like the heavy ones of their ancestors but are in fact made of light, wash-and-wear fabrics dyed black? It is perhaps a slight change, but indicative, I think, of the future. So on a more profound level—no matter what happens to outward dress—Judaism in Israel as in America will eventually be modified somewhat from what it was in eastern Europe, perhaps most of all in some of the intangible ways to which I alluded earlier. It may not happen dramatically, and it certainly will not be an utterly new departure, but the "music's" performance will gradually change in both places. So has it always been.

JL: But isn't the "music" of American Judaism ultimately more likely to resemble Reform or Conservative Judaism? They certainly seem to have adapted to America more than the Orthodox.

AA: But they have changed the notes. They have altered the sheet music, taking out whole sections of it and saying, "We don't need to play this part"—much of it, really—while transposing other sections into a different key or inserting whole phrases and motifs from another piece. This was a grave mistake, and one that has worked terrible damage on the fortunes of Judaism in this country, transforming it (in the worst extreme) from the service of God to the service of man and "ethnic identity." I do not say this with any pleasure or satisfaction, because I know something of the history and original intentions of these groups.

Branches

JL: But you yourself are Orthodox, aren't you?

AA: I have never liked the term, to be truthful, though I suppose that in America one must be stuck with one label or another.

JL: What do you mean?

AA: Certainly you must know that, up until rather recently, there were no "branches" of Judaism at all and that, indeed, in most parts of the world today (including Israel), there is basically only one "branch," that is, Judaism. And so it was with us – no one in my family ever claimed to be "Orthodox," only Jewish.

JL: Is that so?

AA: These splinter movements belong only to certain parts of Europe and to America. I admit that to someone like yourself it must now seem only natural that Judaism come in three or four varieties, but believe me, for most Jewish communities in the world the idea is utterly strange. In Aleppo, of course, we knew nothing of this – and perhaps for that reason, I am still able to look at all sides with some sympathy, if not quite objectivity. But in the end you are right: I believe, with the "Orthodox," in sticking to Judaism as it has been and holding to our traditions – without this there is no Judaism at all. And I hope that eventually everyone will see this, for the situation as you know it in America is less than a century old.

JL: Actually, I don't know much about the history of it.

AA: Reform Judaism started in Germany as a result of the Enlightenment and, later, the political emancipation of the Jews in the nineteenth century. The full story of its origins is rather complicated, involving as it does a host of factors in the political and intellectual history of the Jews; but basically one can say that Reform sprang from a desire to modernize Judaism and reconcile it with both the new rationalistic tendencies in European thought and with the challenges, and possibilities, of life in an increasingly open and secularized society. In premodern times, as I said, the Jews of Europe and elsewhere had existed largely as communities unto themselves; in the eyes of the common people and of the king (and consequently in the eyes of the law as well), Jews were often viewed as a wholly separate entity, a people within a people, with their own restrictions and obligations. This could be a pernicious arrangement or a relatively harmless one, but it was in any case largely unquestioned—at least until the rise of modern times. When, in the late eighteenth and nineteenth centuries, Jews in western Europe began increasingly to have the option of entering the mainstream and eventually of even being, for example, both "good Jews" and "good Germans," some Jews felt the need to redefine the significance of their being Jewish in the process and even to alter the Jewish religion itself. This effort found various forms of expression, one of which was Reform Judaism.

JL: But I take it you don't approve of what resulted.

AA: Well, I should say first of all that anyone can sympathize with the inner struggle that helped to bring about Reform's rise. Nor, truthfully, was this the first time that Jews had sought to redefine their beliefs or practices in keeping with general changes in the intellectual and/or political currents of their day—in fact, such redefinition has been a leitmotiv throughout Jewish history. But in the case of Reform, the mistake they made was to abandon the foundation. There were many Reformers who simply wanted to turn their religion into a "Mosaic" version of German Protestantism, complete with German hymns and stately organ music, and the rejection of all "distinctive" practices (which meant not only the elimination of such things as Hebrew prayers and kosher food laws, but virtually the destruction of our whole *halakhah*). Reform Judaism was not transplanted successfully to much of eastern Europe nor, for that matter, to too many other places on the Jewish map, but it did become a powerful force in America where, if anything, it at times assumed an even more radical guise. Some American Reform congregations eventually ended up forbidding such practices as the wearing of skullcaps, and even held their weekly services on Sundays so as to be more like their non-Jewish neighbors.

JL: I know, but wasn't some of that only natural? I mean, you have to consider things in their historical circumstances.

AA: Of course. The founders of Reform certainly thought that they were doing good for Judaism, and in any case they were, as I say, only responding to the extraordinary pressures of their changed situation. And I certainly do not think that there is anything to be said against those who nowadays espouse Reform, many of whom know no other way. But you must nonetheless look at the present with open eyes and understand things for what they are. For once you have some notion of what Judaism really is, once you understand what it means to live fully the life of our *halakhah,* then these branches of Judaism must appear to you as they do to me, a deviation, "new things recently come," as it says in the Torah, "which your forefathers esteemed not." And the more that these branches seek to sever themselves from the trunk, I am afraid, the more withered and lifeless they must become. However much the Brooklyn Hasidim you mention may be ill-adapted to life in America, they at least have something that is alive, they know what it is to seek to serve God with their lives. And the same is true of my own community, the Syrian Jews in New York (though we have no such beards or coats), and of many others. In contrast to these, however, not a few home-grown American Jewish institutitions seem to be concerned only with what is called "Jewish survival," a rather melodramatic name for the hope that future generations of American Jews will continue to see themselves as such, will marry other Jews rather than Gentiles (though even this has ceased to be more than a mild desideratum for some), and will perhaps even maintain some institutional link with Judaism, a synagogue or Jewish center or social organization. But seen in such terms, the whole undertaking seems quite sterile and unappealing, virtually an invitation to future generations to do otherwise. For what is the Jewish people without the core, the Jewish religion and traditions, our devotion to God and the path of Torah?

JL: To hear you tell it, it sounds like American Judaism is doomed: either it lives in little ethnic communities that resist Americanization, or it dies as soon as it becomes truly American. Is that what you think?

AA: No, not that, though the picture is hardly rosy. And yet it seems to me that in the past, Jews have always faced such challenges of adaptation in new places and environments, and they have nevertheless managed well. In fact, it has often occurred to me that what the Reformers in Germany and here have truly accomplished is the stifling of just this process.

JL: How so?

AA: By jumping over it. Had there been no Reform, I am certain that the pressures that created it would instead have served to mold Judaism within the framework of our *halakhah,* not only in modern Germany but in America as well. That is to say, in seeking to remain faithful to our traditions, but within the context of an entirely new set of social and political circumstances, they would have arrived at a "music" both new and yet consistent with our *halakhah.*

JL: You mean there would have been another movement devoted to modernization within the old framework.

AA: Perhaps not a movement, since the history of these is not an inspiring one, particularly in America. In fact, your formulation is rather similar to that first announced by the other main branch in America, Conservative Judaism, which, as its name implies, was in part a reaction against Reform, an attempt to "conserve" far more of what it called "historical" Judaism than the Reform movement had.

JL: I didn't know that.

AA: Yes indeed. Again you must see things as they developed in time. For one of the things that Reform had done was to crystallize a movement opposed to it—this was where so-called Orthodoxy came from, a nineteenth-century reaction to Reform. It was a rather ragtag affair, joining under one roof (more or less!) Orthodox spokesmen from highly Westernized communities, principally in Germany and Austria-Hungary, with simple traditionalists, heads of yeshivot, religious politicians, Hasidic "rebbes" with their hundreds of followers, and so on and so forth. It was no simple matter to homogenize these elements—in fact, no homogenization ever took place—but some of the diversity in these various communities and factions fell victim to the common cause against Reform.

JL: So you're saying that the middle ground was abandoned, only to be taken up by Conservative Judaism.

AA: It was not so simple. Although it too has European roots, Conservative Judaism is essentially an American phenomenon and has to be understood against the background of the great influx of eastern European Jews to this country that we mentioned, at the very end of the nineteenth century and the beginning of the twentieth. At that time, Reform Judaism loomed large on the American horizon. The relatively few Jews who were already here, by and large the children or grandchildren of German peddlers and merchants who had immigrated in the middle of the nineteenth century, were often quite alienated from strict adherence to Jewish practice in any case and had adopted Reform with great enthusiasm. But the new immigrants at the turn of the century were of a different bent and quite suspicious of both the Reform doctine and those who espoused it. At the same time, they, or rather their children, were in something of a bind with Orthodoxy. Many religious Jews had chosen to remain in eastern Europe rather than emigrate to a country where such practices as Shabbat and the dietary laws were difficult, perhaps imposssible, to maintain; this meant that those who did come were, however attached to traditional Judaism, generally willing to compromise on some of its particulars, at least in the short run. The result was an immigrant generation that was somewhat schizophrenic. Many of the them, despite the demands of their new environment, did remain true to the religion of their past, organizing themselves into communities and synagogues—often based on their countries of origin or even individual cities and towns of origin. If some of them were obligated to work on the Sabbath, they nevertheless sought to maintain their affiliation with Judaism as they had known it. Thus, their synagogues were overwhelmingly what you would call Orthodox. But as a whole, these little congregations they founded in America died when their founders did, or changed radically. For a variety of reasons, the immigrants were largely unable to pass the old ways on to the next generation. Of course the "generation gap" was not a small factor in this: the native-born generation (that of your own grandfather, I imagine) tended to look down on its parents' Old World ways, their accented speech, their relative ignorance of American life. These children tended to view Judaism, at least Orthodox Judaism, very much in the same terms, as ignorant and old-worldly.

JL: And so they became Reform Jews, or Conservative?

AA: Not yet. Reform continued to be viewed with suspicion, even in the next generation, although it did make some inroads. As for Conservative Judaism, it was just now beginning to emerge as a major force. So at first these Jews remained affiliated with some Orthodox synagogue or other, perhaps even starting new ones in the new neighborhoods to which they moved. But it was often more a case of attachment to the traditions of their aging parents or to the Judaism of their own youth than the result of their own commitment to our *halakhah*. Indeed, some who belonged to these synagogues did so only in order to have some place to go for Rosh ha-Shanah and Yom Kippur, or a place in which to say the Kaddish.

JL: Well, then, what about Conservative Judaism?

AA: Conservative Judaism had, as I said, begun independently, and only grew rather slowly at first. It saw itself as a "modern" Judaism, but one historically connected to the great Jewish past, and at first it seems to have aspired to wooing Jews away from Reform and back to the norms of traditional Judaism. It wished, in fact, to be *the* Judaism of America, in which all factions could learn to coexist. Although it was from the beginning somewhat of two minds, its official stance was initially quite compatible with, indeed virtually indistinguishable from, Orthodoxy.

JL: But it soon changed?

AA: Not all at once. The differences between Conservative and Orthodox were for a long while concentrated on relatively trivial matters, some of them even what might be called matters of style, as well, of course, as on the very fact that Conservative Judaism set itself apart as a separate movement and one that, in theory at least, contemplated some accommodation to Reformist tendencies. Beyond these, there was a certain lack of strictness with regard to *halakhah,* but this was hardly the result of doctrine issued from the top, at least at first. I believe it is an old joke about the Jewish Theological Seminary, Conservative Judaism's rabbinical college and spiritual center, that it consists of a group of Orthodox Jewish professors teaching Conservative Jewish students how to be rabbis in congregations that are largely Reform in temper. This is only a slight exaggeration, or it was until a few decades ago. In fact, to catch up on our story, many of today's Conservative congregations are lapsed Orthodox ones. For while the second-generation Jews remained traditional for a time and belonged to Orthodox synagogues, after a time many of them became affiliated with the Conservative movement, and many whole synagogues changed camps. To some it seemed simply like the modern, nay, the *American,* thing to do, an affirmation of their being both Jews like their parents and yet (unlike their parents) fully American as well. And, in terms of *halakhah*—at least at first—the changeover must have appeared relatively minor. In fact, in the same period some Orthodox-trained rabbis also switched over and became affiliated with the Conservative movement.

JL: What for?

AA: For just the same reasons. And, of course, they also wished to keep step with the congregations that they intended to serve. But perhaps the greatest factor for many Jews at this time was the generation gap I mentioned, and a certain social pressure that went with it.

JL: How so?

AA: I mean that the choice to become a Conservative Jew, or some-times even a Reform Jew, for that matter, was often not so much the choice of a particular ideology, nor even of a particular kind of syna-gogue service, as it was the choice of a certain social caste. For as time went on, it became clear that those who remained closest to the reli-gion of the Old Country were by and large those who "stayed back" in other respects as well: they continued to live in the same old neigh-borhoods after others had moved out, they still inhabited a largely Jewish world, still spoke Yiddish on the street and in stores, and so forth. To be Orthodox soon became a statement about one's unwill-ingness, or inability, to step out into the larger American society—and, to a great extent, about one's own economic success in the new world, since opportunity lay beyond the confines of the ghetto. The result was that, for two or three generations, Orthodoxy in America was symbolically associated with the least Americanized, least prosperous segment of American Jewry.

JL: But isn't that inevitable? I mean, even today?

AA: I don't know. I am, as you say, "Orthodox," and my experience at least suggests that our *halakhah* can live in America as it has in so many other places. I do not wish to be glib. Certainly not too long ago it *was* difficult both to keep Shabbat in America and to run a busi-ness or even hold down a job. But now at least this is not the case.

JL: But if that was the case not too long ago, how can you fault previ-ous generations for leaving Orthodoxy?

AA: I told you, I see no purpose in faulting what is history, only in describing things as they are now. But I am saddened by things as they are now, for these groups have changed much since those early years. It is not only that Conservative Judaism has now come to cut itself off from traditional Judaism and *halakhah* in a way that would certainly astonish its own founders, and that it has gradually led many of those formerly Orthodox congregations that affiliated with it into practices that they could hardly have contemplated when they first changed over. But more subtly, and devastatingly, I think, Conservative and Reform Judaism together have come to present to the next generation of American Jews an image of Judaism, of the Jewish religion and way of life, that is so flimsy, a pale reflection of the real thing. It would be better, I think, for the same Jews who pray in such congregations to come into contact, if only once or twice a year, with a living, breathing Judaism than to be able to segregate it utterly out of their lives as they now do, mentally bracketing it as another "branch" of Judaism that has nothing to do with them.

And in the failure of this to happen, in America and elsewhere, I cannot but think that the attitude of the Orthodox—again, for historical reasons that are quite understandable—has been no small contributor. Let me put it clearly. I have been, in Aleppo and Paris, in Sephardic communities whose individual members vary greatly in their adherence to our *halakhah*. It is not an ideal situation, I will warrant, and yet I find it a healthy thing that neither the strict nor the lenient in these places ever proposed ousting the other or starting their own "branch" of Judaism. I even recall one synagogue in which some people used to come on Saturday morning and, at a certain point in the service, discreetly disappeared. Everyone knew that they were going to their jobs. Of course this was not right and was not approved of, yet if I properly understood the attitude of those who stayed, it was generally not one of condemnation so much as mild sympathy, even pity: "Poor fellows, they find themselves in circumstances in which they must work instead of enjoying the day of relaxation and celebration as we are accustomed to do." And, as I say, it never would have occurred to anyone in the synagogue to say to them, "If you cannot stay until the end, please do not come at all, because you are a corrupting influence." Nor did it occur to any of those who had to work to go on and found a new "branch" of Judaism based on the dubious proposition that work is permitted on the Sabbath.

JL: And this is what happened in America?

AA: It is my impression that both things have occurred here, and in a curious way they have cooperated with each other, so that Reform and (later) Conservative Judaism, kept at arm's length by an Orthodoxy valiantly trying to hold the line, felt still less tied to Judaism-as-it-had-been, and so began a course of changes that ultimately have severed them entirely not only from American Orthodoxy, but from Jews in Israel and around the world.

JL: Your Parisian synagogue may be a nice model of tolerant pluralism, but I wonder what would happen if, instead of it being a few people who slink out halfway through the service, fully three-quarters or nine-tenths of those present left to go to work. That is to say, it seems to me that something like Conservative or even Reform Judaism was just inevitable in America. You yourself admit that the America in which one can be both Orthodox and a functioning, integrated member of society is a relatively new, and (who knows?) perhaps evanescent phenomenon.

AA: Perhaps. My point, in any case, is certainly not that history should be undone. What happened happened. But just as we must consider the causes, so we must consider the results. And the sad truth is that these new "branches" have distorted Judaism in the way that I described. And it is all the more a pity because a whole generation, at least in America, has now grown up with the impression that all this is somehow normal, that there are indeed "branches" of Judaism, or degrees of holding to our *halakhah*. It seems to me that this is the greatest harm, that many Americans think they know what it is to be a Jew, when in fact they know nothing of the sort.

Prayer

JL: I can see what *you* find wrong with Conservative and Reform. But certainly they're okay for some people. They're better than nothing, and that's what most people would have without them.

AA: Perhaps, although my point was precisely that through their very existence they have created a barrier between most American Jews and Judaism as it always was, Judaism as a way of living. But in any case, my concern is not with them but with you, Judd. And I would love to go on chatting with you, but I sense from some of what you have said that it may be to no purpose.

JL: What do you mean?

AA: After all that we have talked about, I am afraid that you really don't seem terribly committed to pursuing this on your own. And that is all right, believe me. I am not out to kidnap you into being a Jew, even if that were possible. Perhaps sometime later, a few years from now, you may be more interested in trying to start.

JL: No, I'm interested now, that's not true. It's just that there are only so many hours in a day —

AA: Please, this is a lame excuse.

JL: — And besides, as I say, I'm not really sure that the framework–I mean, the university, the courses–is really ideal for me.

AA: But I told you, it will never be ideal. You will just have to make do with what is available until you find something more suitable. But perhaps indeed you would make out better in one of those yeshivot for people who are just starting. Of course, this is a big commitment. And from what I can tell of you, even there you probably would not find your classmates ideal.

JL: No, I just want to learn the way I can now, step by step. You yourself said that that was the way to do it.

AA: Yes, but you have to *do* it, you have to begin.

JL: But I have begun, at least mentally; really, I have been thinking about it a lot. . . . Look, you know what I'm interested in, I'm interested in poetry. I like to read it—which is not very common these days—and I write it, and even write about it. Because for me, it all seems so open, it's a whole world. But in a way I think that's also what makes me interested in Judaism, and this is what I've been thinking about. Because it also seems open to me, a large, open tradition. No doubt this sounds pretentious. But let me put it in terms of the same comparison that you were making before, between Judaism and writing poetry. If I were to try to say what the two have in common, I wouldn't necessarily put it your way at all. Because, first of all, the thing that strikes me about poetry is that nobody invents it. What I mean is that there is this activity, writing poetry, with its own tradition and rules and, most of all, lots and lots of poems that have already been written. And what you do, when you start writing, is really to pick up this idea, which you didn't invent, and try to make it your own, or make yourself part of it—in a sense, to give yourself to this tradition that already exists. Perhaps you're not aware of it at first. At first you're only interested in doing something that comes out of yourself. But the way to do that, you come to see after a while—the only way to do that, because you didn't invent poetry, as I say—is to investigate further, to understand more of what it is that you have inherited and taken on. So you read other poems and find out what other people have done up until now, even technical things like what they have done about line breaks and different shapes of poems and meter. Do you see what I mean? So I think that's one of the things that attracts me, you know, to Judaism; I think it's similar, at least, with regard to tradition and starting new.

99

AA: Well, Yehuda. . . .

JL: Another thing about poetry, of course, is precisely this idea of a framework. Because poets need that too: there is absolute freedom — you can say anything, really — but on the other hand that's exactly why you need something, some shape or frame, in which to get started. Do you see what I mean? And there's also something even more basic, although here I hope you won't find the analogy offensive. You asked last time about inspiration. The thing is, there is also a tradition to that. If you go back to Homer or Vergil, you have this standard convention, the "invocation to the Muse." The poet starts off his poem by asked the Muse to inspire him. Now this may be, at least in some such texts, merely conventional; but certainly there was a reality that went with it for many poets, a reality that stands behind the convention in the first place. Lots of classical poets really imagined — "knew," they would have said — that there was someone out there, some real Muse, who *gave* their poetry to them. Even such a rational fellow as Plato says this, in fact, he claims that the poet's brain is simply "taken over" by the inspiring god and used for the purpose of writing a poem. This was not a small thing for him to say. And it wasn't just in ancient Greece or Rome. Many later poets — in the Renaissance, the seventeenth century, the Romantics — have described things in just these terms, right up to our own day.

AA: I don't really see what you're getting to.

JL: All I'm getting at is this: nowadays perhaps psychiatrists or whatever would talk about this in terms of "projection" or "command fantasies" or some other delusion, and maybe in some cases they'd even be right. But the point is that for a lot of poets, or maybe all poets, this is where the poetry comes from. Do you see what I mean? There is a real reality behind the framework, and perhaps the best, the truest way to talk about it is indeed in the old terms, and not to get hung up on what's "inside" the poet's head and what's "outside." Because once a poet is willing to surrender to this old way of thinking, he is free in a certain way, precisely because he knows, or is willing to entertain the possibility, that what he is going to write down is not, or

100

might not be, what he alone decides to write. Do you see what I mean? I think that's really what this "Muse" has been doing all these years. And look at all the beautiful poems she has brought into existence!

AA: I'm not sure that that has much relevance to our subject. In fact, what you say is somewhat amusing. It reminds me of the old joke about the fellow who goes to the psychiatrist complaining that his brother believes himself to be a hen. "A common fantasy," the psychiatrist says. "Bring him in to see me and I can cure him in a few sessions." "I may eventually do that," the brother says, "but for now we still need the eggs." You seem to want to defend the idea of a productive illusion–but I can tell you, there is nothing illusive in that way in Judaism.

JL: I'm not saying there is, in fact, I'm not even saying that about poetry. All I'm trying to do is explain how–I mean, from my point of view —

AA: Then perhaps you will permit me, from mine, to explain why merely thinking the things that you are thinking will not advance you very far. So let me tell you something about the business of banking. The basic wherewithal of banking is, as you know, money. Now in our society, as in many different societies, including even very primitive ones, money plays a crucial, if somewhat underappreciated, role in people's lives. So in America, for example, workers work hard at a job, sometimes even a job involving some personal risk or physical suffering, and they are paid for their trouble at the end of the week with some pieces of paper that have green printing on them; these are called dollars. (In fact, as things go nowadays, people are usually paid with a check, that is, another piece of paper, which itself only represents the issuer's intention to pay out those first pieces of paper, the dollars). Eventually this worker goes into a store; there the owner of the store allows the worker to walk out of the store with vegetables and milk and so forth that have been brought there from a farm somewhere, again, at the cost of considerable physical toil and hardship– allows and even encourages the worker to walk off with these valuable goods and takes in exchange for them some more pieces of paper with green printing on them.

JL: I get the idea.

AA: Do you? Because this is just the beginning. I have said nothing about money's other functions—how people seek to accumulate it and invest it, how it is loaned out, via various institutions, by thousands and millions of little individuals and thereby enables great buildings or even whole cities to rise from the ground up, or how enormous projects are undertaken with it that would otherwise be quite unrealizable—in fact, how our whole world, as we know it, is entirely dependent upon our money system and would collapse in a day without it and reduce us all to the meanest and most primitive way of life.

JL: But what's the point?

AA: Just this. Imagine for a minute that you are a man from Mars come to investigate life on earth. You would see all the things that I have described, the exchange of goods for little pieces of paper and so forth, but none of it would make any sense to you. You would want to know why people keep on accepting these pieces of paper and storing them up in banks and so forth; you would ask whether these dollars are a particularly durable and versatile food to be eaten, or if perhaps they contain some high-energy substance that can be inserted into a slot to drive a motor or something similar—and, of course, my answer to you would have to be no. "But they must have some intrinsic value," you would say. And all I could tell you is that their value is indeed quite real but is based on nothing that you can see with your eyes or touch with your hand. For this is precisely the case with money in our modern economies.

JL: What's the point?

AA: The point is that you are now similarly perplexed, because you are still a Martian. You see the things that we do and you say, "Why that?" "How could anyone undertake such a thing?" And you are especially perplexed because all the things that you see are similarly held together by something quite intangible, something that is neither edible nor capable of driving a motor nor even able to be put on a scale and weighed. You cannot understand these things from the outside, because from the outside you can only see with your eyes, and what you see with your eyes will not give you the slightest clue. You see activities, cities being built, but what is essential you cannot see. And here the analogy ends, so let me speak in real terms. You must learn to see from the inside, Yehuda, you must let your heart guide you into a world that is not made for the eyes. And for this the way is prepared, as I have said; but you must start down it. Otherwise you will always be perplexed, you will always be standing on the outside. Now, I suggest that you go back and think about these things. And certainly I do not know what is in your heart or where it will incline you. Perhaps you will not want to continue; that is perfectly fine. But if you do wish to go on, then I think the way is clear. It is the way I have told you about, with Shabbat and prayers and Hebrew and the rest.

JL: Will you tell me about prayers?

AA: But I have already told you. You must learn them, in fact, you must learn them by heart so that you can always say them, effortlessly, three times a day, as I explained.

JL: But you didn't say why they are so important. Unless of course you are tired of talking about things altogether.

AA: No, I will tell you. Prayer, you see, is what we offer up to God, and our offering, like the sacrifices that were offered in the Temple, should be perfect. This is another reason why you should concentrate on learning the prayers by heart.

JL: Yes, but this also is a little unclear. Because if you say "prayer" to most people in America, it means asking for things, or perhaps meditating, but not offering something.

AA: But with us it is different. Not that we do not ask for things in our prayers, but even this asking is also form of service.

JL: I don't follow you.

AA: It goes back to the sacrifices I mentioned. While our Temple still stood in Jerusalem, the *kohanim* (that is, the priests who served there) would offer up sacrifices every day, animals and sweet-smelling incense.

JL: I knew that, though I must say it has always struck me as a little primitive.

AA: It was a gesture.

JL: I beg your pardon?

AA: It was a gesture, in fact *the* gesture, the principal form of worship. Some day, perhaps, we may discuss this, but for now it is necessary only to understand that this was the way things were. Each day in the Temple in Jerusalem, Israel would make such offerings to God and so serve Him; this was our most direct and constant gesture. And then, when our Temple was destroyed and sacrifice was no longer possible, it was as if this reaching out to God might no longer be possible either. Yet there did exist another gesture, another form of contact, which was well known to everyone, and that was prayer. And so our Rabbis established prayer in place of sacrifices, as even the prophet had earlier proposed, "And let our speech take the place of sacrifices."

When I say that prayer was established in place of the Temple service, I mean it quite literally: in the Temple, sacrifices were offered twice a day, early in the morning and again toward evening, so corresponding to these it was established that Jews should say the words of a special prayer, the *Amidah*, twice a day, early in the morning and again before sunset. (In fact we say it a third time, after sundown, to correspond to yet another daily event in the Temple routine.) The *Amidah* is *the* prayer in Judaism, and our whole prayerbook is really structured around it and the obligation to say it every day.

JL: What does it say?

AA: It originally consisted of eighteen little sections (nowadays nineteen) of a sentence or two each. For that reason, by the way, the prayer is also called by some the *Shemoneh Esreh,* the "Eighteen."

JL: What are the sections?

AA: Well, to begin with, do you know what a *berakhah* is? It is a fixed formula used in our prayers, usually translated "Blessed art Thou, O Lord. . . . "

JL: I know that. Although it always struck me as hubris for human beings to "bless" God—shouldn't it be the other way around?

AA: Quite so. The translation is faulty, though for understandable reasons. What the Hebrew really means is something like, "I praise and thank You, God . . . " But rather than put ourselves first in the sentence, we express it more modestly in the passive: "Praised-and-thanked are You. . . . " Now this word "praise-and-thank" in Hebrew also carries the sense of the English word "bless," which is why this formula is sometimes translated "Blessed art Thou" or "Blessed are You." But as such, "bless" really means something closer to "wishing or sending all good things," and so it can work in either direction, we can bless God—wish, as it were, "all good things" to Him in gratitude—and God can also bless us.

JL: I see.

AA: Now this formula, "Blessed are You, God . . . " is the basic building block of most Jewish prayers, sometimes introducing them, sometimes concluding, and often both. In fact (as you will learn), *berakhot* are entirely formulaic sentences—I have only given you the way they begin—with only a word or two differentiating the *berakhah* for one occasion from that for another. We use these *berakhot* as a ready formula of thanks, and there are fixed ones to be said before eating or drinking or enjoying anything of this world, or before performing this or that *mitzvah.* These *berakhot* you can find easily in a prayerbook. Now the daily *Amidah* (as you will see in the same prayerbook) consists of eighteen, or rather nineteen, *berakhot* in a row—we begin by praising God in somewhat general terms in the first three *berakhot* and then ask, one by one, for the main sorts of things that all Jews

105

everywhere might be expected to ask God to bestow on them—understanding, forgiveness, health, prosperity, etc., as well as the restoration of our national fortunes—praising Him at the same time for these gifts. The *Amidah* ends with our acknowledgment of God's power over us and a renewed request for His blessing.

What is the trouble?

JL: This idea of formulas has to be a little disturbing. I can understand that Jews are supposed to pray at certain times, especially if the prayers are supposed to correspond to the old sacrifices. But it seems to me that prayer, if it's going to have any meaning at all—shouldn't it be something a little more personal, straight from the heart? The minute you start talking about formulae and fixed this or that, don't you kill the whole thing?

AA: Yes and no. It would obviously be so if the recitation of the prayer became nothing more than a rote exercise, but such a prayer is in any case considered unacceptable in Judaism. On the other hand, the existence of formulae and, in fact, a fixed text is of great advantage. For prayer is, as I said before, a reaching out to God: in the *Amidah* we stand before Him ("standing" is, in fact, the meaning of the Hebrew word *amidah*) and speak. Now at this moment we must (as I once described to you) have absolute certainty; our standing there and reaching out must flow of itself, and the words must come out uninterruptedly to make a great line, a connection, between us and God—that is why we must be entirely collected and sure of where we are going. And so it is that the content of our prayer, and eventually each and every word, came to be fixed, lest we wander and lose our way.

JL: But then why call it prayer at all? It really sounds more like some kind of ritual reciting.

AA: But in the case of the *Amidah,* much of what we actually do say is what even you would call prayer, that is, *asking*—as in this list of things I just mentioned, understanding, forgiveness, health, and so forth. Our prayers contain requests as well as praise precisely to prevent their recitation from becoming mere rote: in asking for these

106

things before God and realizing that it is from Him that we receive them, our whole heart and everything that we are and need can go into our words and so travel mightily.

JL: But this is only true of some of the *berakhot?*

AA: Yes, as I said, the beginning and end of the *Amidah* contain praise of God and acknowledgment, and these are in fact the invariable part of the *Amidah.*

JL: I thought the whole thing was invariable.

AA: Not precisely. I mean that there are "special editions" of the *Amidah* that are used on Shabbat and holidays; these are different from the weekday one I have been describing. On Shabbat and holidays the beginning and ending *berakhot* are, as I said, the same, but in place of the middle ones are substituted one or two having to do with the Sabbath or the holiday in question.

JL: Why is that?

AA: Both because it would be improper to turn our thoughts to our daily needs on Shabbat, and because we actively wish to connect our words to the fact of Shabbat or our holidays, which is inevitably so much on our minds on those days.

JL: As usual, the situation seems to be getting more complicated.

AA: It really is not. As I said, the whole prayerbook is built around the *Amidah* and the obligation to say it every day, three times a day. Once you learn the daily *Amidah*—which you will learn just by saying it, at home and in synagogue—then the slight differences between it and the Shabbat one will be easily mastered. In fact, although it is not a requirement, I think that you must eventually memorize the whole thing, for the reason that I said. Although it is not so common nowadays, for most of our history Jews knew all the prayers by heart; prayerbooks were not, as now, distributed to those who came. And so people simply learned, by dint of repetition, to say the whole service by heart.

Speaking of repetition, did I mention that the *Amidah* is usually recited silently – standing, of course – by everyone, and then repeated out loud, in the morning and afternoon services, by the one chosen to lead the prayers? This gives us a chance to say the *Amidah* ourselves as individuals standing before God, and then to stand as a community and repeat, through one voice, our common request. What is more, this repetition will soon help you, if you concentrate, to learn the whole text by heart, and you will thereafter be able to turn to God unimpeded. And what is still more, as I said, you will have the key to most of the prayerbook as a whole.

JL: "Most"?

AA: The other requirement, beside daily recitation of the *Amidah*, is one that you already know, the requirement to say the *Shema*. Although these two things might logically be separate, it has long been our custom to join them together. And so our morning service (called in Hebrew *Shaharit*) is built around the *Shema*, with special *berakhot* before and after it, and then the saying of the *Amidah*; the afternoon service, *Minhah*, consists just of the *Amidah*; and the evening one again combines the *Shema* and its *berakhot* before and after with the saying of the *Amidah*. This is basically our way of turning to God, three times a day every day. Once you master it you will never be lost in a synagogue.

Klein and Gross

JL: There's something else about prayer, though. I'm sure you'll take offense at this and tell me about standing on the outside again. But couldn't you tell me something about what it's like, I mean, what it's like to actually be saying the prayers you're talking about?

AA: Why should I take offense, Judd? But you are right: this is another question from the outside. What can I say? Only what I said before: there is a way to enter, there are details, and this is how you must go. The details help you, they are the pitons on the mountainside.

JL: But why can't you just say what it's like? You certainly must know the answer—can't your mouth just say the words?

AA: It is not I who am the trouble, but you.

JL: What do you mean?

AA: Let me see how I can explain it to you. . . . It has to do with two Jews, Klein and Gross. Gross is very fat—or, rather, he overlaps his outline, like a child's drawing, do you know what I mean? When a child draws a picture, first he makes the outline, a circle for the head, larger circle for the body, and so forth; then he colors it all in. But this is difficult, the crayons are hard to control, and so the shirt's red jags out beyond the outline, and the cheek's pink here and there juts into the sky. It is in this manner that Gross is fat, he overlaps, and as a consequence he is always getting in the way of himself. Even if he tries to whirl around very quickly and see what is behind him, all he will actually see is the part of himself that overlaps whirling around to meet him. Klein, on the other hand, is small. Not physically small, but discrete, held perfectly inside his own outline. And so he can see and walk about in a different way.

JL: I see. And so you are Klein and I am Gross.

AA: Not at all. Klein and Gross are the same person.

JL: I don't understand.

AA: Gross is the way we are. I do not know why it is so, perhaps it is connected to evolution, but it is the way we are. And it is a fine way to be, swashbuckling at times, save that it is quite unreal, this overlapping, and so hinders us from what is real. That is why I said, the trouble is with yourself. You wish to rush up to that which is *kadosh,* holy, and pick it up and examine it. But this has never been done. Gross and *kadosh* cannot meet.

JL: Why not?

AA: Because Gross will walk right by. Or, if he is very lucky, Gross will turn into Klein.

JL: What does it mean to be Klein?

AA: I told you, to fit within your borders and be small.

JL: Are you talking about ego loss or something like that?

AA: Don't be silly. I'm talking about something physical, fitting inside your borders.

JL: Can I become Klein?

AA: But this is still Gross talking! Certainly—send in some breakfast cereal box tops. But make sure you print your name clearly.

JL: Seriously.

AA: Haven't I told you that there are steps, that things come in a certain order? In the days of the Temple, one who wished to approach *kadosh* had to be pure, and there were special purification procedures to be followed.

110

JL: And now that there is no Temple?

AA: But I have told you about the *mishkan,* have I not? And I have told you how we immerse ourselves in Torah, and I have told you that our prayers are like the offerings that were made of old on the very altar. Do you see?

JL: I guess so.

AA: No you do not. But it does not matter. You will have to go the way I said or you will not go at all. To anyone but an American this would be clear.

JL: I am still thinking about Klein. Can't you tell me anything more?

A Lawnmower

AA: No, I would rather talk about *halakhah*. This is really where I think you need to get started. You have so much to do here, to learn and to do.

JL: What more is there? I think I understand the basic idea— *halakhah* has to do mostly with what prayers to say when, what to do on Shabbat, and so forth, isn't that it? But as far as learning it all is concerned, I suppose you're right that the best way for me to begin is just to be around people who know these things.

AA: Quite so, at least at the beginning. And yet, I'm not sure you really do understand the concept. Judaism is, as I said, all about serving God. But from the beginning this service has consisted of keeping the *mitzvot*. So it is that in the Torah, as I once mentioned, where the injunction to "love" or "serve" or "fear" God appears, it is frequently further defined as, specifically, "to keep His *mitzvot*," indeed, all "His laws and statutes and commandments," or simply to "walk in all His paths." And the *mitzvot* in the Torah include all manner of things, not only things like prayer or Shabbat, but many other things, including relations between human beings.

JL: But it seems, at least from what you've said so far, that that side of *halakhah* has a sort of secondary place in Judaism —

AA: Certainly not. In fact, if you knew something more of the way Jews really live, you would know what a central role these things have, including what Jewish children are taught in school.

112

JL: But we were talking about *halakhah*. *Halakhah* itself, you'll admit, seems to be very much taken up with ritual.

AA: Not at all. *Halakhah* is, as I once explained, our path, all the practical, down-to-earth ways in which the *mitzvot* are applied to daily life. We have so far talked about *halakhah* in such areas as Shabbat and prayer, but we can as well talk about "Honor your father and mother" or "You shall love your neighbor as yourself" and their application.

JL: What application? I mean, once you've said it, you've said it.

AA: Not at all. You see, you still don't understand about *mitzvot*. The *mitzvot*, as the Torah itself observes, are no empty matter, but are "your very life." In other words, in every way possible our lives are to be shaped by the *mitzvot*, and so we must be very precise in the way we understand and carry them out. They are not merely a good idea, and not even merely a general guide.

JL: For example?

AA: Examples are, in fact, one of the ways in which the application of the *mitzvot* is sometimes defined. Thus we have a verse in the Torah that says *lo tikkom velo tittor et bnei 'ammekha*, "You shall not take revenge and you shall not bear a grudge against your countrymen." But what does this mean?

JL: I don't know.

AA: But if you don't know, how can you keep this *mitzvah*?

JL: Well, I guess it sounds fairly straightforward. I think I know what revenge is.

AA: Well, for example, aren't there cases for which revenge is justified? Or indeed, what constitutes revenge? Suppose, for example, my lawnmower breaks down and I go to borrow yours, but you say, "Mine's really a very delicate machine, I'm afraid I can't lend it out." Then, suppose that next week you come over and ask to borrow, say, my hedge clipper, and I say, "You didn't lend to me, why should I lend to you?" Would you say this constitutes a violation of the Torah's prohibition of revenge?

JL: It sounds sort of petty to qualify as revenge—I should think that would be reserved for blood feuds and the like. . . . I don't know, I suppose it all depends on your motives. I mean, if revenge is forbidden and you're doing it for revenge, then I guess the answer is that you are violating the commandment.

AA: Quite right. But the point is that the Rabbis discussed and illustrated the *mitzvot* in just these concrete terms, so that there would be nothing abstract about them. By the way, my example is almost the same one presented by them, save that in place of "lawnmower" and "hedge clipper" they said "scythe" and "spade." Now in thinking in these down-to-earth circumstances, the Rabbis were anxious to insure that the *mitzvot* would come to *intrude* in our daily lives in a hundred different ways, so that, in trying to negotiate a particular situation, we would not simply have our eye on the situation itself or on our own potential gain or loss, but that we would see ourselves in the larger framework of the Torah and never have it far from our thoughts.

JL: Yes, that's what you've said before. And what you describe is sort of appealing, on the one hand, I mean, having rules for this or that situation. But I have to say it also strikes me as a little totalitarian as well. After all, life is a fluid thing, and I'm a little suspicious of the kind of personality, frankly, that wants to have everything pinned down in advance, "In such-and-such a situation you do such-and-such." Do you know what I mean?

AA: You mean you're in favor of *halakhah*, so long as it doesn't impose itself on daily life.

JL: That's not fair. What I'm talking about is really a kind of personality—the sort that has to know in Situation X exactly what to do or say in advance.

AA: Perhaps. But I think that, precisely because life is, as you say, fluid, things can never really be pinned down in advance; besides, the

114

type of personality, or rather attitude, that this approach of our *halak-hah* suggests to me is rather different. It belongs to people who, as they go through life, seek to direct their thoughts and deeds to Heaven, so that, no matter how caught up they are in the things of the moment, they are never far from larger things, that is, they are never so caught up that they cannot stop and consider themselves and their situation from the standpoint of the Torah.

JL: Well, let me mention the other misgiving I had about what you said. Because your description really strikes me as being at odds with what one sees in the real world.

AA: What do you mean?

JL: To listen to you, one would think that Jews—no, that religious Jews, the ultra-Orthodox—would *ipso facto* be paragons of morality and righteous conduct. But just open the newspaper and you'll see that that isn't so. I'm sure you recall a little while ago the famous Jewish philanthropist who was convicted of insider trading violations on Wall Street —

AA: I don't believe that fellow answers to the description of Orthodox Jew —

JL: Well, if not him then I'm sure you could find others who *were* Orthodox, even pillars of the Orthodox community. How can you reconcile —

AA: Perhaps, but a rotten apple or two should not discredit the whole —

JL: It's not a rotten apple or two I'm talking about. Frankly, my impression of Orthodox Jews in general is that they just aren't the sort of people who interrogate each and every action for its moral implications or worry about questions of ethics a whole lot. I may be wrong, but that's my impression.

AA: If it is, perhaps there is something behind it. But I must tell you that I have a different impression. I have lived with traditional Jews from various communities and in different countries. And I admit

115

that with us you will not find much public posturing over this or that issue. But what you will find, at least what I have found, are people who, as a habit of daily life, try not to speak ill of someone else—anyone—because this too is part of our *halakhah*. And people who do not lie or steal. Under any circumstances. There is a kind of straightness there, quite understated, "perfunctory," you might say, but one far more real to me than all sorts of public moralizing which often does turn out to be mere posturing. Apart from this I should say that the whole world of those old Yiddish-speaking communities—their "style," to use a current term—must seem quite foreign to you, as it still does to me. What seems understated, or unstated, in their way of being may be unstated precisely because there is no need, because they understand each other. What I find characteristic of Jews—ordinary Jews, in many different communities—is a fundamental decency of the sort that one could not take for granted in other groups. And this is true too of those old eastern European communities and their descendants here. In any case, your business is not to be them, but to learn from them how to be a Jew and uphold the same *halakhah*, and to do that ultimately in your own fashion. And this, to return to our subject, still means knowing about lawnmowers, and the difference between vengeance and holding a grudge.

JL: Was there a difference for the lawnmower?

AA: Yes indeed. Don't forget, the verse in question said, "You shall not take revenge and you shall not bear a grudge. . . . " What do you suppose the difference is?

JL: Well, I don't know the precise meaning of the Hebrew words, if they do have a precise shading. I suppose it sounds as if the two are really part of a single idea. In English, in any case, seeking revenge and bearing a grudge are fairly close, though revenge is more the action that you take as a result of bearing a grudge. I guess bearing a grudge is strictly speaking internal, at least in English.

AA: Not in the Torah. In fact, your description of grudge bearing sounds more like what the Torah calls, only a verse or two earlier, "hating your brother in your heart." (That too is forbidden, by the

116

way.) But grudge bearing is something different, and, incidentally, it is a principle of the Torah that nothing is said without purpose, so that if two different things are mentioned, revenge and grudge bearing, then two different things are being prohibited. In fact, our Rabbis defined grudge bearing via the same example of the scythe, or lawnmower, if you will. The first instance, where I say to you, "You didn't lend me your lawnmower, so I'm not lending you my hedge clipper"—this is vengeance. But if I do lend you my hedge clipper, but at the same time say, "I'm lending it to you in spite of the fact that you were so stingy with me only last week . . . "—this is called bearing a grudge. It too is forbidden. Because our obligation is to treat each other kindly and with respect, and if we are wronged to make objection at once. These too are *mitzvot* and cannot be treated lightly.

JL: So what isn't *halakhah?*

AA: Now that's a better question—for really, many, many aspects of ordinary life, whether it is Shabbat or holidays or prayers, or how one behaves with one's neighbors or family, one's obligations in business dealings or in disputes, one's duties to the poor and to the community as a whole, how one is to react in time of adversity or loss (Heaven forbid) as well as in happy times—all this, and still more, is part of our *halakhah*. The basics, as I said, you will pick up quickly, but once you learn how to study you can begin to see where our *halakhah* comes from, what things are derived from which verses and in what manner, as well as to know many nuances that you might otherwise miss.

JL: So by "study," what you really mean is the study of *halakhah*.

AA: No, that would be incorrect. Traditionally, the word *halakhah* has a fellow, and that is *aggadah:* the two together constitute a description of the material one studies, for example, of what is to be found in the Talmud.

JL: And what is *aggadah?*

AA: I suppose the best definition is: anything that is not *halakhah*. But this is hardly descriptive. *Aggadah* is connected to the Hebrew

117

word for "narrative," and is frequently used to refer to the way the Rabbis commented upon narratives found in the Bible. You see, they did not make general comments, "We learn such and such from the story of Joseph," but they were interested in each and every word of the story—much as they were interested in each and every word of the *mitzvot* in order to understand fully the implications for everyday life. In the case of narratives, they wanted to make sense of every little detail of the story and to establish connections between one thing and another.

JL: Sounds like literary criticism.

AA: Lehavdil!

JL: What does that mean?

AA: It means, literally, "to distinguish," that is, let us not compare sacred things with the ordinary. Not that there may not be lines of resemblance between the way the Rabbis explained a text and that of a critic, but there are certainly more differences than similarities. In any case, all this you can learn—perhaps we will discuss it later. I only wished to say that our Rabbis sought to interpret and apply everything in the Torah, and that which seeks to establish our own practices and behavior is *halakhah,* whereas *aggadah* is, as I said, generally connected with the interpretation and elaboration of narratives.

JL: And is subject matter their only difference?

AA: There are other differences that derive from this main one. *Halakhah,* as you will see, is often very down-to-earth, whereas in talking about narratives and seeking to make connections, *aggadah* is sometimes highly creative. It is also, incidentally, sometimes quite humorous, in a way that I hope you will come to appreciate. In fact, you can see how the two really complement each other, and why they were included in nearly equal measure in the Talmud.

118

Korah

JL: Can you give me an example of *aggadah*?

AA: I am sure that you know some *aggadot* already. Are you familiar with the little booklet we read at night around the table on Passover, the *Haggadah*? (The name *Haggadah*, incidentally, is merely the native Hebrew form of the originally Aramaic *aggadah* – the two are the same word.) In any event, this book is full of *aggadot* – the Four Sons, the unreported plagues at the Red Sea, and so forth – these are actually clever expansions on an interesting little detail or two found in the text of the Torah.

JL: What details?

AA: Well, that would be long to tell. Perhaps I should start instead with something simpler, an example from this week's *parashah*. As you know, every week a successive portion of the Torah is read in synagogue, so that the entire Torah is read in the annual cycle of readings. Incidentally, one of the things Jews have traditionally studied during the week is the Torah portion (the *parashah*) for each upcoming Shabbat. And by "study," of course, I mean we do not just read the Torah itself, but the traditional commentaries on it as well.

JL: Which are?

AA: In olden times, Jews read the Torah along with an Aramaic translation of it, not only because Aramaic was then the everyday language of many Jews, but because the translation, or *targum,* was often somewhat free, going out of its way to explain difficulties in the text. So the custom in those days was each week to read the Torah portion

119

itself twice and the targum once so as to gain an understanding of it. There also were, as I explained, verse-by-verse commentaries on biblical books, known as *midrash,* and one could also study these in detail. Then, in the Middle Ages, a number of outstanding scholars wrote or compiled new commentaries. The best known and most popular of these was Rashi's commentary. Rashi was a talmudic scholar who lived in France in the eleventh century. But how can such a central figure be described? He was an extraordinary talmudist, perhaps the greatest of all times, and, in fact, he wrote a commentary on the Babylonian Talmud that is still the standard guide to that text, published in virtually every edition of the Talmud since. That commentary in itself was a lifetime undertaking, but he somehow found the time to write commentaries on the biblical books as well, and his Torah commentary has achieved a similar preeminence among Jews everywhere. In it he took many of the interpretations passed on by the Rabbis and known to him from targum, Talmud, and various midrashic collections, selected the ones he wanted, and put them all into a running commentary on the Torah, adding here and there interpretations of his own.

JL: And why was his commentary so popular?

AA: Because it synthesized a great deal into few words, and because it selected its material so as to be both internally consistent and to eliminate many troubling, albeit charming, elements of earlier midrash. The commentary was not only an instant classic, but ultimately it changed the way Jews all over the world studied biblical texts. It soon became the favored practice to study the Torah with Rashi's commentary, sometimes exclusively so. And so today, you can easily find an edition of the Torah that consists of the text itself, the Aramaic targum of Onkelos, and Rashi.

JL: And the other commentators you mentioned?

AA: If you knew Arabic you might well study the Torah as we did, with the Arabic translation of Rav Saadya Gaon, a Jewish scholar of the tenth century. Indeed, just as common as are editions here of the Torah plus Onkelos plus Rashi, so were editions of the Torah plus

Onkelos plus Saadya (sometimes also with Rashi or others)—the Taj, or "crown," we called them—in my youth. But in addition there are other medieval commentaries, those of Abraham ibn Ezra or Naḥmanides, that one can also study. Indeed, sometimes these are all printed together in editions called *Mikra'ot Gedolot*, great anthologies of biblical commentaries printed side by side.

JL: And what about *aggadah*?

AA: Aggadah, as I said, is really a general term with various uses. But basically I am using it here to refer to midrash, that is, interpretation, of narrative parts of the Torah—what is in fact sometimes called *midrash aggadah* as opposed to *midrash halakhah*, or interpretation of legal material. This week's Torah reading is about a figure named Koraḥ, who seeks to foment rebellion against Moses during the Jews' forty years of wandering in the desert. Now if you were to limit yourself to reading the biblical account, you might have any number of questions about Koraḥ: Why did he stir up this revolt? What were his motives and his methods? What are we to learn from the Torah's account?

JL: And this is what one would find answered in *aggadah*?

AA: Well, yes, this and more. But perhaps I should make clear that *midrash aggadah* is a general category of interpretation, a critical concept rather than an actual book. The book in which you would look to find this form of writing might be a midrashic collection, like *Midrash Rabba* or *Midrash Tanḥuma*, or indeed Rashi's commentary, which, as I said, selects much material from the writings of the Rabbis.

JL: I see.

AA: Now another thing that I should try to impress upon you is that midrash in general, whether interpretation of legal or nonlegal material, is a kind of interpreting that will at first seem foreign to you. It takes a while before you get the hang of it.

JL: How so?

AA: Well, to begin with, you have to develop some feeling for the Torah as the Rabbis saw it. They had studied it from early childhood on and knew its words almost by heart. So it was simply a fundamental "given" in their lives: every little turn of phrase, every slight odd detail in the text, was enormous and imposed itself on their consciousness. Now in thinking about such things, they did not, as modern commentators do, seek to explain the Torah as if it were just an ordinary, human text. Each detail was potentially significant, and in trying to unfold that significance—especially with *aggadah*—they therefore sometimes felt justified in proposing highly creative solutions, connecting one detail with another far removed from it or inventing whole conversations or incidents not in the biblical text, whose existence might then help explain the particular odd word or phrase upon which they were commenting. In other words, midrash is a form of interpretation, or textual commentary at least, but one that is very different from any you may now know, precisely because it is commentary on a sacred text.

JL: I see.

AA: But the hardest thing to convey about all this is the *flavor* of *midrash aggadah.* For the Rabbis, the biblical text is a certainty, it is *there,* whereas their own explanations and elaborations have a kind tentative quality—"Well, this is one possible way to make sense of things. . . ." (I am speaking now about *aggadah.* For matters of *halakhah,* of course, it was necessary to define things clearly and definitively, and for this, of course, the Rabbis could rely on the traditions handed down orally from ancient times.) With *aggadah*—well, here too they had ancient traditions, but there was no real necessity to define once and for all the significance of this unusual word in the story of Joseph, or that apparently unnecessary repetition in this speech of Abraham's. And so collections of midrash often pile up three or four explanations of the same problem side by side, as if to say to the reader, "You choose."

From what I have said you will understand another strange thing about midrash, and that is its apparently narrow focus. It typically seems interested only in explaining a single verse rather than a whole story (and even when its interest is the whole story, it attacks this topic via one or another particular verse). This is certainly a difference between it and other forms of interpretation. Indeed, as I said, it is not just the verse, but most often little peculiarities in that verse—an unusual turn of phrase, say, or an apparently unnecessary detail or repetition. For example, in the matter that we discussed before, "You shall not take revenge and you shall not bear a grudge," the Rabbis assumed that these two things simply could not be judged to be the same idea in different terms, or the second used for purposes of emphasizing the first.

JL: Why not?

AA: That is just the way rabbinic interpretation works, the way of learning the most from the text: everything in the Torah, every peculiarity of expression, is there to teach us something. And in assuming this, midrash, of course, will find an ample supply of things that require explanation. In fact—although it might sound a little ironic—perhaps the most helpful thing that I can say at this stage about midrash generally is that it ends up elucidating a lot of difficulties that probably would not have bothered you in the first place. In other words, your normal tendency would probably be just to go along in the *parashah,* following the main thrust of the story or the *mitzvot* being set forth, and so make your way through to the end. And this you could certainly manage without our commentaries. In fact, what the commentaries do is rather to force you to slow down and consider every little detail—why this word and not that? What is the connection between this and that, or what is the distinction? And of course such questions are never asked in any particular case unless the commentator has in mind a good answer.

JL: Like the difference between revenge and grudge bearing.

AA: Exactly. Or let me give you an example from the beginning of this week's *parashah:* When Korah is first introduced to us, in the very first verse, his name, and that of his father and grandfather and great-grandfather are all given—a very full introduction!—but there the genealogy stops. This stop might appear all the more striking since, if

123

this list of ancestors had continued back only one generation more, it would have arrived at Jacob himself, Koraḥ's illustrious great-great-grandfather.

JL: So why didn't it?

AA: This is exactly the question the midrashists asked—and, as I said, they never asked a question unless they had a ready answer. In this case, they said that the reason is to be sought in another verse elsewhere in the Torah—in fact, several books away, in *Bereshit,* Genesis. At the end of that book, Jacob is about to die, but before he does he blesses each of his sons in turn. In speaking there of Shim'on and Levi, he introduces a discordant note; he says, "Let me not come into their counsel, nor take pleasure in their assembly." Do you get the point?

JL: Not at all.

AA: Well, what could Jacob have meant by these words? That he didn't approve, in some measure, of those two sons is clear enough—still, "not come into their counsel nor take pleasure in their assembly"?! Did he wish never to see them again? Hardly. And so our Rabbis understood these words as a subtle allusion to the *descendants* of Shim'on and Levi (for Jacob was held to have had prophetic gifts in these last words of his and was in fact contemplating his children's descendants). And in the case of Levi—or so at least our rabbinic interpreter assumes—he must have foreseen that four generations later would be born a boy named Koraḥ who would rebel against Moses. It was upon foreseeing this that Jacob would thus have said, "Let me not take pleasure in their assembly"—that is, even though I will be long dead, I want it known that I do not derive any satisfaction from this rebellion of my descendant, nor do I approve of it. So in deference, as it were, to his wishes, the Torah in introducing the incident traced Koraḥ's genealogy back to Levi, but not to Jacob, Levi's father.

JL: I see.

AA: Not quite. Because I have not yet told you what saves this explanation from being merely farfetched. In Jacob's sentence back there to

Shim'on and Levi, he used the word *kahal* for "assembly." This is not an unusual word in Hebrew—still, it is a somewhat strange thing for Jacob to have said, "Let me not take pleasure in their *assembly*." Now in the story of Korah, the same root word is used to describe the beginnings of their rebellion, *vayyikkahalu 'al Mosheh*, "they assembled against Moses." So, for the midrashist, this similarity in wording seals his case: Jacob said, "Let me not take pleasure *in their assembly*" in the sense of "in their assembling against Moses," as it says in our story. Do you follow?

JL: I think so.

AA: This example illustrates another thing I mentioned about *aggadah,* indeed about midrash in general: it is very much interested in the interrelationship of one verse with another, even if the verses are separated by several chapters or, in this case, are from different books. Because the point of view of midrash is that all of Scripture is a single, essentially seamless, text, so that the key to understanding a particular detail in one of the stories of the Torah may lie in a verse in the Psalms, or in the book of Chronicles. Indeed, midrash apparently derives great satisfaction in establishing some not-very-obvious connection between two rather remote things.

JL: I see.

AA: I could say more. That satisfaction is a large part of midrash. Because ultimately the point of midrash, whether *midrash aggadah* or *midrash halakhah,* is not only to make sense of the text at hand but to make us aware of the harmoniousness of Scripture as a whole. Sometimes this is no easy task, for apparent contradictions abound. And so the midrashists, and we ourselves, take great pleasure when two things, such as Jacob's last words in *Bereshit* and the omission of Jacob's name from Korah's genealogy, can be so cleverly brought into line by the appearance of the common term *kahal.*

And I should perhaps add that cleverness in general is the great hallmark of midrash, especially with regard to *aggadah,* the interpretation of narratives such as that of Korah's rebellion. You see, these interpretations, although we now teach them to schoolchildren from the time they begin to study Torah, are very much aimed at mature minds and sensibilities; many of them are redolent of the atmosphere of the ancient study-house, where they were discussed and passed along by scholars who had lived their whole lives with the Torah and its occasional puzzles. Consequently there is often something rather sophisticated, arcane, and frequently not a little facetious about the sorts of questions they ask, especially about biblical narratives, or the answers they give. I hope you will get a feeling for *aggadah,* and especially for this curious mixture of earnestness and irony, which seems to me so distinctly Jewish.

JL: Is what you're saying that *aggadah* is basically concerned with connections of one passage with another?

AA: Not merely that, no. There are many different sorts of things that midrash seeks to answer about the text, and many different ways it tries to go about doing it. Sometimes, as I said, the midrashist supplies, out of his own imagination, details or whole episodes that are "missing" from the Bible itself. In fact this happens precisely in regard to Korah: For the biblical text tells us that Korah had a whole band of followers, but it really never tells us how he got them or what he said to them to persuade them to follow him in this rebellion. But our traditions, as passed on by the Rabbis, supplied a story that fills in the gap. They said that Korah began by posing questions to Moses in such a way as to make him appear an arbitrary and autocratic leader.

Korah's first question, according to this tradition, was about the law of fringes: As you may know, the Torah requires that every four-cornered garment come equipped with corner fringes dyed a special blue, as a visible reminder to Jews everywhere to keep the *mitzvot.* (This, incidentally, is the origin of the *talit*—the "prayer-shawl"—worn in synagogue, although its fringes are not blue anymore: the precise substance from which the blue dye used to be made is no longer known and so is nowadays dispensed with.) Korah said to Moses: If there were a garment which itself was entirely dyed this special blue, would the law still require that it have this special blue fringe? After all, if it is this blue dye that is supposed to call to mind the *mitzvot,* would not an entire garment dyed blue fulfill the reminding function far better than just the corner fringes? But Moses answered no, the blue corner fringe is still required. Koraḥ then asked a similar question: If there were a room filled with copies of the Torah, would not such a room be exempt from the requirement of having a *mezuzah* on the door (the *mezuzah,* you must know, is a little oblong box affixed to the doorpost containing a small part of the Torah written on parchment). Again Moses answered no, the *mezuzah* is still required.

JL: And these questions showed Moses to be autocratic?

AA: Well, somewhat, by making Moses' decisions appear to be illogical. But there is a deeper meaning to these stories, one connected to what Koraḥ really does say in the Torah. For the precise claim he makes there against Moses in starting his rebellion is that Moses is lording it over the Israelites without reason. "This whole group is holy," he says in the Torah, "with the Lord in our midst—why then should you be exalted over the congregation of the Lord?" Do you see how, on the basis of this wording in the Torah, Koraḥ could be depicted as having asked just the sort of question that he does in these rabbinic stories?

JL: Not really.

AA: Well, the question about the garment that is entirely blue is really only a metaphorical representation of Koraḥ's literal claim. For if, in place of "blue," you read "holy," you will understand that for Koraḥ, there is no more need for Moses to be singled out as special than there is need for a special blue corner fringe on a garment that is already entirely blue. And, by the same logic, in a room full of sacred books there would be no need for a special *mezuzah* on the doorpost—the contents of the room itself are certainly as sacred as any *mezuzah.*

JL: Now I see your point.

AA: So in asking these questions of Moses, our tradition shows Koraḥ to be a somewhat more subtle figure than he might appear if one were to read only the bare outline of our biblical story. He presents himself to Moses very much as a student might to a great rabbi, asking, as it were, erudite questions of *halakhah*. But—as is sometimes the case in real life—the questions were not motivated out of a desire to learn. And that too, I suppose, was an important lesson to impart both to students and teachers.

JL: I see.

AA: But that is not all, for in transmitting precisely these stories, the Rabbis were answering another question, the sort that might not bother you at first, but one that was very much on their minds. For one question that midrash often seeks to answer is why one thing in the Torah comes before or after another. This is really the flip side of the interest midrash has in connecting or reconciling two related, but distant, verses in the Bible; for here its aim is to understand the connection between two apparently unrelated, but adjacent, items in the Torah. For example, it might wish to know why, in the Torah, the law concerning a woman taken prisoner in warfare is followed immediately by the law of inheritance in a polygamous marriage, and that by the law of the rebellious son.

JL: And what's the answer?

AA: You will probably come to it in time. But for the present, can you guess why it is that Korah begins by asking his question about the corner fringes?

JL: Was it that the law of corner fringes immediately preceded the story of Korah in the Torah?

AA: Bravo!

Jacob

AA: All this is very nice, Judd, but I have to say, it will mean nothing unless you finally start in on the business of being a Jew.

JL: Don't worry, I'm going to go on. I would like to "see the world as Jew," as you say. Although even today I think my understanding of what that means is a little different.

AA: I take it you mean that you realize now how much is involved before you can begin to see what it's like.

JL: Not really. On the contrary, I think that's what I'm starting to get now. Certainly I think I know why learning is such a central thing in Judaism (and why, for that matter, learning of all sorts therefore became a sort of Jewish preoccupation in the modern world). I think I even have some feel for the flavor of Jewish study. In any case, I know about *halakhah* and *aggadah* now.

AA: But just now you do not sound particularly happy to have learned all this.

JL: No, I'm happy about it, or at least, as I said, I would like to go on. It's only that in some ways I wonder if studying is not somehow beside the point, or at least could be. Because everything you say about study and the "service of God" seems now to exist only in potential. And I understand why this should be: study is, as you say, a commandment of the Torah, so if people study, they fulfill the commandment, whether they are thinking about the "service of God" or not. Do you see what I mean? Studying Torah, or I suppose lots of other things, can just become a kind of autonomous activity, so that in doing them you can lose sight of the whole purpose in the first place. Or am I back to what you call jogging?

AA: No, what you say is very true and has been said before. Perhaps this is a hazard in other ways of living as well. In any case, the matter that you raise is a central one for Jews, a matter of the heart, which we call by the Hebrew word *kavvanah. Kavvanah* is usually translated as "intention," though often it means more precisely intent*ness*, that is, the participation of the heart in an action. For as I once said, the *mishkan* makes open a space, a regular possibility, in the heart. And yet despite this, sometimes there is no heart in the performing of a *mitzvah.* The *mitzvah* becomes mechanical, and the heart is not there. This can happen with one *mitzvah* or, perhaps, many. In the extreme, it may be possible for someone to keep Shabbat, study Torah, say the prayers, and so live fully within the framework of our *halakhah,* and yet for these to become only a routine and no more. I believe it is unlikely, in the long run, because to do these things requires a willing heart. Still, as I said, in the end the *mishkan* is only a possibility. You know, it is a *mitzvah* on Rosh ha-Shanah to hear the sound of the shofar being blown. Our Rabbis asked: What happens if a person chances to be passing by a synagogue at the time the shofar is blown? Is the fact that he heard the shofar considered as a fulfillment of the *mitzvah?*

JL: And what's the answer?

AA: The answer is that it depends on his heart. *Im kivven libbo, yatsa', ve'im lav, lo yatsa'.* "If he directed his heart to the *mitzvah,* then he fulfilled it; if not, he did not." It follows that two people can perform precisely the same action – in this case, two can hear precisely the same sound coming from the same shofar – and yet their acts will have two entirely different significances. I do not wish to go into all the issues connected with *mitzvot tserikhot kavvanah,* that is, the role of intentionality as a matter of Jewish law, on which, in any case, there are differing opinions. But in regard to the question as you have posed it, it is the heart and heart alone that is decisive.

JL: But then I come back to what I was saying before. You talked about "seeing the world as a Jew." Yet now, by your own admission, there may be plenty of Jews, even Jews who are for all the world strictly observant of *halakhah,* who nevertheless have nothing of the view of things that you describe.

AA: Certainly it is not up to you or me to look into their hearts. For people are deceiving in this way—they may bluster about, they may seem crude and even worse than crude in their behavior, or they may seem intent on performing *mitzvot* only for self-satisfaction or self-congratulation. Yet what is in their heart when they stand to say the *Amidah,* or what is in their heart at any time, it is not my business to guess. In any case, even if their hearts are empty, what difference should it make to you?

JL: Maybe none. But what you're saying now makes it seem that the *mitzvot* might really be just a side issue. If everything depends on the heart, then let the heart go its own.

AA: But the two go together. So in the example that I gave, there are two elements: the sound of the shofar, and the heart that aims to hear it and fulfill the *mitzvah.* If the heart is not there, as I said, then the shofar is just another sound, lost in the beep of daily traffic, and the *mitzvah* remains unfulfilled. But if the shofar is not there, then all you have is the heart, listening in vain to the sounds of traffic, groping about without direction. It may be that the *mishkan* is only a place, a possibility, but that is a lot.

JL: But doesn't the *mishkan* do anything besides just being there? It must also shape people's thoughts.

AA: Well certainly, living according to our *halakhah* must also do that. And then there is another thing, but it is hard to describe.

JL: What is it?

AA: A certain attitude, one that arises from the heart directing itself in the way I said. The attitude itself is thus a by-product, but still very important. And how to describe it? I guess it is somewhere between realism and humility, neither optimism nor pessimism, but perhaps exhibiting a bit of both simultaneously, if that seems possible. Per-

131

haps I can best illustrate it with the words of our ancestor Jacob when he was returning from a stay of many years with his uncle Laban in Aram. Just then he found himself in a very tough situation. He had left Laban after an angry dispute, so the road of return to Aram was effectively cut off to him. At the same time, coming to meet him was his brother Esau and a company of armed men, who, Jacob feared, might be bent on harming him and his family, perhaps killing them all. What to do? Yet when he turned to God – the same God who had told him to leave Aram and was thus, so it might seem, very much responsible for his present fix – what were Jacob's words? *Katonti mikkol haḥasadim umikkol ha-emet asher ʿasita ʿim ʿavdekha.* "I am not worthy of all the kindnesses and all the faithfulness that You have bestowed on Your servant." Do you see what I mean? A cynic might say that Jacob was simply, as it were, preparing God for a new request, that he now be saved from danger. But I do not think so. I think his words were quite sincere, and they bespeak in a funny way the outlook, that other aspect of "seeing the world as a Jew," that I am trying to describe.

JL: I see.

AA: When we set our hearts on performing the *mitzvot,* it is as if we ultimately have a different perspective on things. In the case of Jacob, it is certainly that, despite the crisis of the moment, he was able to look back over his life and all that had been granted to him theretofore. But I think it is more concrete than that. In turning now to God, he is no longer the brash young man he once was – a brashness that was apparent, I think, when he first encountered God at Beth-El. Indeed, the contrast between that moment and the one I am describing could not be more striking.

JL: How so?

AA: Now it is as if Jacob is more confident – or perhaps not exactly more *confident,* because he is of course frightened by his situation. But he is somehow given over to God in a way that he was not before. He is no longer making vows, offering deals – he has played his last card long before. And so it is, I think, with our *halakhah*: once you are committed to it, you can only walk down the path all the way. And, walking down it, you cannot but have a sense of God's overwhelming bigness in our lives.

JL: Bigness?

AA: Yes, that is really it: the Jacob of this moment in the story seems truly to have *shrunk* vis-à-vis God. And so perhaps it is no accident that he expresses himself as he does. *Katonti mikkol ha-ḥasadim* means literally not "I am not worthy of all the kindnesses," but "I have become small from all the kindnesses." This too, I think, is an important part of the Jewish way of seeing.

PART IV

The time: some months later

"Physical" Mitzvot

AA: Well, Judd, I was glad you could come by. How are you coming with your study of Judaism?

JL: I've kept up with the courses. And my Hebrew is certainly getting better.

AA: Good. What shall we talk about this afternoon?

JL: I didn't come with a list of subjects. Really, I think most things are pretty clear. Although there are a few random topics I haven't gotten around to tracking down myself. For example, what is the rule about wearing a *kippah* on your head? I know that it's required in synagogue, but why do some people also wear them outside?

AA: I should answer first by explaining the origin of the custom. In ancient times, and really up until the present in some places, it was considered a sign of self-confidence, bordering on arrogance, for a person to go about bareheaded. For example, in the Torah, when the Israelites left Egypt, the text says that they went out "with hand held high," that is, proclaiming their victory. When Onkelos sought to translate this into Aramaic in his targum, the clearest rendering he could think of was "they went out bareheaded." This for him well captured the feeling of the Hebrew expression.

JL: I see.

AA: And so it was customary, as a matter of personal modesty, not to go about bareheaded. In one place the Talmud observes that a person must not strut about in a ramrod posture, nor ought he to go any distance outside with his head uncovered. Hence the practice of keeping one's head covered outside the house—though of course there was nothing specified about the form of covering. In Aleppo we wore ordinary hats, and so I do today. Those little skullcaps were developed, as far as I know, relatively recently, in Europe, as men began also to cover their heads consistently inside as well. And frankly, I think it is a good thing. Although the connection with modesty has long since disappeared, keeping one's head covered is both a constant reminder, to ourselves and anyone else who may notice, of our Jewishness and our devotion to God; and it is, as well, a way of keeping faith with the traditions of our ancestors. For a long time, of course, many Jews in this country hesitated to wear a skullcap in general society, and even today some find it impossible to wear one all the time. But I see many young men nowadays, not only students but also doctors and accountants and storeowners, who go about with *kippot* with no apparent difficulty.

JL: And in synagogue they are absolutely obligatory?

AA: Some head covering, yes.

JL: What about women?

AA: Women in Judaism are likewise to behave modestly, and this used to mean some kind of head covering. It was always our custom for married women, and even girls after a certain age, to cover their hair, just as among other peoples in the Middle East. But standards of modesty are constantly changing, and this makes setting immutable standards difficult. In America I have noticed that women who are otherwise strictly observant are sometimes less stringent about this nowadays.

JL: Don't you think the custom might change for men too?

AA: Perhaps, although, as I said, the trend seems to be in the other direction. But I will tell you in general my philosophy about such matters, which I think of (though I admit somewhat inexactly) as "physical" *mitzvot*. I prize them, precisely because they *are* physical, involving an utterly tangible object or some relatively simple, unre-

138

flective act. You know, some of the other *mitzvot* that we have discussed, such as not speaking ill of other people, are quite nuanced
and also require great vigilance and mental effort; *teshuvah*, repen-
tence, and similar concerns are likewise sometimes very challenging.
They should not, for all that, be slighted; on the contrary, these
"duties of the heart" (as such *mitzvot* have been called) occupy a central place in our *halakhah*. But, perhaps for that reason, when one
comes to physical things like covering one's head, or wearing the
small *talit* —

JL: What's that?

AA: Don't you know about the *talit kattan*? It is like a small under-
shirt, really just a four-cornered piece of cloth with a hole for the head
and those corner fringes we mentioned on each corner. We wear it
under our shirt, as a way of observing the law of corner fringes (which
only applies to such four-cornered garments) while still being able to
wear other, ordinary clothes over it.

JL: I see.

AA: That is another *mitzvah* that really requires no effort, and yet it
stays with us all day, something physical and uniquely our own. And
so with other physical *mitzvot*. By now you certainly know about the
tefillin that we strap on our arm and head during the morning prayer.
This too is something that we do and it is done, a clear physical token;
and even after they are removed, the imprint of the *tefillin* stays with
us for some time. And so with the other physical things, not only
things that touch us physically, but *mitzvot* such as the *mezuzah* we
put on the doorpost: you nail it up once, and forever after you pass
it by and see it, and there it is, a physical token to turn your thoughts
from the everyday to God. You will understand what I mean when I
say that these really embody for me the whole philosophy of our
halakhah, a way of giving the heart a concrete, physical form of
expression.

JL: What other "physical" *mitzvot* are there?

AA: Well, as I say, this is an unofficial category of mine, whose borders are not easily defined. But within it I would also group, for example, many of the *mitzvot* connected with our holidays. On Sukkot we take up the *lulav* and *etrog* in synagogue, and we sit inside the *sukkah*—these too are physical things, and there is a special feeling that attaches to doing them, to performing such a tangible act that is connected to the very words of the Torah.

JL: What about the laws of kosher food?

AA: Well I suppose that they are similar—they too certainly have to do with tangible, physical tokens. But they are also in some ways a special case, and one connected with another phenomenon in our *halakhah,* the whole matter of *kedushah,* "holiness." Should we talk about the dietary rules?

JL: Why not? Everybody else does.

Kosher

AA: What do you mean?

JL: Well I have, as you would say, absorbed the essential from my contact with other Jews at the university. But I also can't help noticing that kosher food is the one subject people like to go on and on about, and it gets more and more complicated—what is, what isn't, who's heard what about what. . . .

AA: I cannot deny having noticed the same phenomenon. But let's begin at the beginning. The word in Hebrew is *kasher,* or "kosher," as most European Jews pronounced it. It means "fit" or "proper." Now basically, there are relatively few restrictions on what one may eat. For example, all edibles that grow from the ground, fruits and vegetables and grains, are fine—a strictly vegetarian diet cannot run afoul of our kosher laws. Meat, however, has certain restrictions. To begin with, the Torah contains lists of animals, as well as certain species of fish and seafood, and also various kinds of birds and insects, none of which may be eaten. What it all comes down to is that, in terms of meat, we nowadays basically eat only beef and lamb and most domestic fowl (chicken, turkey, duck, and the like). Moreover—and this is in effect the most restrictive provision—these animals may not simply be mass-killed as they are in the great slaughterhouses but must be slaughtered individually by a *shohet,* a specially trained Jewish butcher. The animals thus slaughtered are then sold to the public in kosher butcher shops, though nowadays certain meats—especially frozen chickens and sausages—are also sold through ordinary grocery stores and supermarkets.

JL: And any of this meat is okay so long as it is labeled "kosher"?

AA: Here are some complications. In most places there are no laws preventing unscrupulous merchants from labeling products "kosher" that in fact are not, so one must rely on brand names. In this case the "brand" is not necessarily the name of the product, but the name of the rabbi or certifying organization that makes sure that the laws have been properly observed. An individual butcher shop (or, for that matter, kosher restaurant) usually has a rabbi who acts as supervisor, or *mashgiah,* for its observance of these laws, and his name is usually announced somewhere on the premises ("Under the supervision of Rabbi X" or "Supervised by Such-and-Such Organization"). More-over, the product itself may contain a label mentioning the rabbi's or organization's name—this is true for mass-marketed goods. There are in fact various kosher-certifying organizations whose distinctive mark—for example, a circle with the letter U in the middle—appears somewhere on the outer packaging of the food in question. You can get to know the various symbols and what they stand for. Then you will be surprised to find them on all manner of things sold in grocery stores—not just meat products, but breakfast cereals and cookies and dishwashing detergents and hundreds of others.

JL: Why those?

AA: As I said, any meat that we eat must come only from certain kinds of animals and must be specially slaughtered and prepared. But many of the things that people buy in stores contain animal prod-ucts—animal fat is sometimes used for shortening, for example, or animal products may be used in cheese or gelatine or margarine, or they may be the basis of certain preservatives—and these things, even if only in small quantities, can render the whole food unfit. So these same kosher-certifying organizations actually inspect the factories and procedures of large mills and manufacturing plants so as to be able to certify that this or that mass-marketed spaghetti or tuna fish is also kosher.

JL: In effect, anything you buy is guilty until proven innocent, that is, not kosher unless specifically stipulated to be so.

AA: Well, not really. As I mentioned, fresh fruits and vegetables are always all right, and so, as a matter of practice, are quite a few other things. I have noticed that in different countries observant Jews are aware of the peculiarities of their location and so may differ from place to place as to what actually requires certification. With this, as with other things, the best way for you to learn is to observe what other Jews who are careful about our traditions actually do. But if you want there are also written guides to the dietary laws that you can buy in a bookstore; these will give a more precise orientation. Besides, there are a few other major elements in the picture that I have so far omitted.

JL: Like what?

AA: Well, for example, I have said nothing about the prohibition against mixing milk and meat products, but this is also one with great ramifactions. Because of a prohibition in the Torah, we do not cook milk and meat together, or milk and fowl—so cream sauces, for example, with chicken, or frying meat in butter, are also out of the question. But more than that, we are very careful not to inadvertently consume the slightest quantity of the one with the other, simultaneously or even separated by a short period of time. Thus after eating meat Jews generally wait before having any dairy product (the amount of time varies by custom, some Jews waiting as little as an hour or others as much as six hours). Moreover, we are careful not even to cook meat in pots used for the preparation of milk products and vice versa, or to serve the one on plates or with silverware used for the other. As a practical matter this usually means maintaining two sets of pots and dishes and utensils, and in fact washing them separately and with separate sponges or scouring tools.

JL: That's what I thought.

AA: Don't worry, though, it is all quite manageable: these rules are observed by thousands and hundreds of thousands of Jews. But I take it, from what you are saying, that you are not yet one of them.

JL: Actually, you're wrong. I gave up eating meat in college—I'm a complete vegetarian. So, as you say, that makes me automatically okay in terms of kosher food.

AA: Well yes, although you still have to be careful about cheese and so forth, as well as prepared foods that have shortening and the like. But if you are a vegetarian, then perhaps you already understand why it is that the practice of *kashrut* has such a strong hold on Jewish consciousness. For it is a fact that, as you say, not only do we talk about it, but even Jews who have in other ways become lax in observing our *halakhah* often remain faithful to the dietary laws. And I believe, although it is somewhat a matter of conjecture, that I know at least part of the reason why.

JL: But honestly, wouldn't you say that for most people it's a relatively mechanical thing that they have just gotten used to doing? That's if there's not a certain one-upsmanship involved—I've more than once heard someone say, "Other people think such-and-such is kosher, but I would never touch the stuff!"

AA: I am afraid that even Jews are not immune to the seductions of "holier than thou": some people do indeed delight in making themselves "more" observant on the basis of imaginary dietary strictures that have no basis in fact. But for all that, I think there is something very positive in the concern of ordinary Jews for *kashrut*—apart, of course, from its role in our *halakhah*. For the fact is that, at bottom, *kashrut* speaks to a central concern in Judaism. But in order to understand it, we must talk about *kedushah,* holiness, and the role it plays even now in our lives.

Kedushah

AA: The word *kadosh* is usually translated into English as "holy," but its meaning in Hebrew is a bit clearer and more precise than the English term. *Kadosh* carries with it the specific sense of "set off" or "made special." So Shabbat is called *Shabbat kodesh* (Sabbath-of-holiness, or "holy Sabbath") because it is set apart from the other days and made special. Similarly, part of the harvest and other things were set aside, dedicated to sacred purpose, and as such became *kadosh*, special—and once special they could not be used for ordinary purposes and had to be treated with great care lest they come in contact with impurities and be rendered worthless. In fact, this quality of "specialness" obtained as well for all that had to do with the Temple. For the Temple itself was *the* sacred place, set off from all that surrounded it and guarded from anything or anyone impure. And so it is known in Hebrew, as *beit ha-mikdash* or simply *ha-mikdash*, "the holy place." Do you follow me?

JL: Yes.

AA: You can see from what I have said already that the idea of "holy" was closely connected to that of "purity." What was impure could not come in contact with what was *kadosh*; in fact, our Rabbis used to use the same root, *k-d-sh,* to express the idea of purifying or washing, for a example a *kohen*'s washing his hands and feet prior to coming into contact with something *kadosh*. And this was because purity and holiness were so closely connected. Now purity in the Torah is a somewhat complicated subject—there were various degrees of purity, and various ways that one could become impure, by contact with dead bodies, for example, or with certain impure substances.

JL: And this is the connection with kosher food?

AA: To begin with, the basis of the food laws as I described them is one of purity: certain animals were considered "pure," *tahor,* and therefore fit for consumption; these are the animals that, if properly slaughtered and prepared, can be declared to be kosher. Food is, in fact, one of the few remaining areas of Jewish life in which the concept of purity, strictly speaking, is still relevant.

JL: Why is that?

AA: Because, as I said, the focus of much of the concern with purity and holiness centered on the Temple, the *beit ha-mikdash,* and all that went on there. When the Temple was destroyed, most of the regulations concerning the Temple itself and its personnel and the sacrifices offered up within it no longer had any application.

JL: Except for food.

AA: The prohibitions against impure food continued, and in some ways one might say that the rules governing the meals of ordinary Jews have become, if anything, stricter over time.

JL: Why is that?

AA: Well this is the point I was trying to get to. You see, I think holiness and purity really have a central role in our religion, even if, nowadays, the Temple itself, formerly the principal focus of these matters, is missing from our lives. The great power our kosher laws have on us—sometimes even when others things have been left to slide—bespeaks something deep within our hearts, perhaps not consciously articulated by most Jews, a desire connected to *kedushah,* be it expressed only in so humble a form as adherence to the kosher rules.

JL: How so?

AA: Well, to begin with, you have to get some of the *physical* sense of purity and holiness, or rather—since the feeling itself may be known to you—come to understand this feeling as part of what is meant by *kadosh.* You see, *kadosh* was, and is, primarily a physical concept. When something was *kadosh* it had to be protected from physical contact with impurities, and when you yourself fell into a state of impurity you could become pure again not by reciting some prayer, but only by immersing your body in a *mikveh*, a bath or stream of running water. Similarly, when the Levites were consecrated for service in the Temple, they were not only sprinkled with waters of purification but, strikingly, shaved all over their body, a physical starting anew; then their clothes were washed and they were made pure.

There is something similarly physical, I think, about *kashrut*. That is why I said I thought a vegetarian might understand. Because instead of just eating whatever comes within your grasp, there are certain rules and distinctions that guide you, so that the very act of eating becomes changed as a result—isn't it so? In a sense, submitting to this regime purifies one's insides in the same way that a bath purifies one's skin, and that physical feeling of purity is unmistakable. As a matter of fact, it is precisely the threat of contracting *impurity*—in the days of the Temple, by coming into contact with some source of impurity, or with regard to *kashrut*, by swallowing some impure substance—that causes one to acquire a sort of self-awareness, even vigilance, as one goes through life, even if, in the course of time, this feeling must become rather routine and second nature. So it seems to me that our zeal for *kashrut* is likewise ultimately a *physical* thing—or, rather, that combination of concrete physicality with things nonphysical that is the essence of *kedushah*.

JL: What do you mean?

AA: Just that: the physical state of *kedushah* in the Torah is also affected by nonphysical things. For if you can think of the state of purity as I described it—almost of being surrounded, as it were, by some sort of separating halo—then imagine further that that halo was capable of being pierced, indeed, dissipated, not only by contact with some external physical impurity, but as well by some moral blemish from within. This is the great principle of the Torah, that our "walking in holiness" depends on our avoidance not only of physical impurities, but the moral equivalent as well. And so the Torah ordains, "*Kedoshim tihyu ... .*" "You shall be holy, for I your God am holy."

147

And this injunction in *Vayyikra* is followed by a long list of impure things to be avoided, some of them quite physical, and others, as I say, involving speech or even thought.

JL: But isn't "Be holy because I am holy" just an instance of what is called *imitatio Dei,* the idea that human beings should strive to imitate God?

AA: I have heard it so described, but I do not believe that to be quite the point, not here. Rather, as our Rabbis said, it is a *kelal gadol,* a great governing principle in our whole *halakhah,* and one to be taken in the most concrete sense. For just as God is *kadosh* and His house, the Temple, therefore had to be protected from anything or anyone in a state of impurity, so the Torah ordains that we ordinary Jews must travel through life similarly separated, sealed off, as it were, from impurity—not only the kind resulting from physical contact with impurity, but impurity of actions as well, or even speech.

JL: But it seems to me that you have to choose: either holiness is, as you say, a physical state, in which case this moral dimension is absent; or else it is not physical, in which case your physical description of it seems wrong.

AA: Perhaps I would state it better if I said that what the concept of *kedushah* countenances is the ability of the moral to, as it were, impinge on the physical, to affect, as it were, one's physical state. And this impinging is witnessed not only in the laws of the Torah, but throughout the histories of the books of Joshua and Judges and so forth, and in the words of our own prophets. So it was, for example, with the prophet Isaiah. When God first summoned him, Isaiah found himself in front of the heavenly throne and was overcome by the holiness: "*Kadosh, kadosh, kadosh*" the text says, "Holy, holy, holy." This is the holiness of God. And what is Isaiah's reaction? "Woe is me, I am undone, because I am a man of unclean lips, and in the midst of people of unclean lips I dwell." It seems to me that these words are most significant for the feeling I am trying to describe. For he felt it even at his lips, felt that the act of speaking—the words that he himself had spoken, as well as even the words spoken by his countrymen which had, as it were, come in contact with him—had been a profanation rendering him unclean.

JL: I see.

AA: And so it is in that sense that "be holy" is the great governing principle of the Torah. In order to carry out this *mitzvah* we must constantly turn our thoughts to Heaven and, as it were, constantly watch our step. In fact, just now it occurs to me that we find the same idiom in Scripture: "Watch your foot as you go to the house of God," it says. Because with that which is holy, you cannot simply bumble along carelessly. So similarly does this expression occur in connection with *Shabbat kodesh*. For while it is not, properly speaking, a place, Shabbat is nonetheless a site of holiness; and so, when the prophet Isaiah wished to warn about guarding its sanctity, he began by using a similar expression, "If you keep back your foot from Shabbat. . . ." And when the Torah says that we ourselves are to be *kadosh*, it is, it seems to me, to be understood that with our very selves we must, as it were, tread carefully.

JL: In more than just kosher food.

AA: Yes. You see, eating is still very much of a physical phenomenon and so speaks to this instinct for *kedushah* quite clearly. But our *halakhah* ultimately leads to the extension of this feeling to other spheres of life as well, until it eventually happens that wherever we go, we walk, as it were, separated off, surrounded by a mandorla of holiness. That is why, as I once pointed out, the "four cubits" of our *halakhah* were compared to the Temple—for our *halakhah*, too, is a site of holiness, but one that can exist wherever we happen to be, pitched right in the midst of our everydayness. And this is the great gift of our *halakhah*, that in following its ways we thereby come to live our lives surrounded in holiness. That is why our Rabbis ordained as a general rule that, before we perform one of the *mitzvot*, we recite a *berakhah* of thanks to God. And what do we thank Him for? *Asher kiddishanu bemitzvotav*—because He made us *kadosh* through the *mitzvot*, and so provided that we walk in holiness wherever we go.

149

Interpretation

AA: But now, Judd, let me ask again. I take it from what you said before that you are going on with Judaism, which is good. But I must tell you again: do not do it halfway. If it is not what you are doing every minute that you are not actually doing something else (and often, even when you *are* doing something else), then you will lose it, this I know.

JL: I understand that. I didn't want to make a point of it, but the fact is that for the last couple of months —

AA: Good. You are a poet, of course. And so perhaps you already can sense how our way ultimately is a way of knowing, in addition to a way of being; that to walk the path of serving God is to know reality, as I once tried to say, in its very details, by its taste.

JL: Yes. .

AA: But then you must obey your heart when it demands more and more of you, as it surely must. Because otherwise you will lose it.

JL: You talk about knowing, and I think I understand what you mean. But then at least some of Judaism seems to depend—outwardly, anyway—on things that seem capricious or on reasoning and assumptions that could be argued with.

AA: Then you do not understand what I mean. There are no assumptions in the knowledge I was talking about; on the contrary, it depends on cleansing yourself of assumptions.

JL: No, I'm not talking about that. I mean, just in concrete terms, that there are a lot of ideas that seem central in Judaism that, from another point of view, might appear eminently arguable: the Torah was given to Moses on Mount Sinai, there is some kind of divine order and justice in the world, and so on and so forth.

AA: These are hardly small matters—nor, for that matter, are the two that you mention questions of the same order. In any case, you are right, we have not talked about them. It is because I have been trying to help you know Judaism from the inside, the Judaism of doing and of the *mishkan*. This is what is truly fundamental. Of course, there is much to say as well about Jewish ideas concerning the giving of the Torah, or reward and punishment, and other things. But as I told you before, the way to begin is with the heart and the *mishkan*; it is by these that you lay the foundation, by the sure particulars.

JL: Yes, but certainly the one is connected to the other. I mean, if the whole *mishkan* is based on the Torah, then isn't it important to know where the Torah came from?

AA: Then know that it was given to Moses on Mount Sinai.

JL: Yes, but what about the things modern scholars say about the Torah—you know, on the basis of biblical criticism and archaeology and so forth. . . .

AA: This is of course an interesting topic. You may as well know that I once set out to study modern biblical criticism in order to gain an acquaintance with it; and I must say, I learned a great many things. I do hope that some day we may be able to discuss it at length. But in order to talk about it, we would have to move very far from the present focus of our discussion; it is not something to be dealt with in short order. So perhaps it is best that we put it aside.

JL: Do you think I should also study biblical criticism?

AA: It is not necessary. What you need to study is Talmud, or the traditional interpretations, midrash and Rashi.

JL: But even here it seems to me that you run up against the same problem. I mean, so many of the things that we do seem to depend on a particular interpretation of a text – the Torah, say – being one way and not another. But I've spent two years in graduate school and four years in college before that, and everything I have studied about literature sets me against the notion that there can ever be something called *the* interpretation of a text. Texts are by their nature ambiguous, open to various interpretations. And yet Judaism seems posited on the idea that we all have to interpret the same text the same way – that that just *is* what it says.

AA: For example?

JL: For example, the Torah says that we should rest on Shabbat – fine. But how do you know that what it wants is for us not to carry our house keys in our pockets on our way to synagogue or to avoid turning on lights or even touching money? Or, on the other hand, how do you know that a lot of the things that we do do are not, in fact, prohibited? All this is just a matter of one set of people having interpreted the text in a certain way. And who's to say that it's the right way?

AA: Well, I might answer you by pointing out, as I did once before, that while any written text is, as you say, potentially ambiguous, it was nonetheless necessary for us as a community to be unanimous in our interpretation of the Torah, at least so far as the practice of it in our daily lives was concerned. For that reason traditions of interpretation were passed on with the written Torah from earliest times, passed on not only in words but in deeds, in ways of doing things. This went on for centuries, until finally our Rabbis codified everything on the basis of these traditions, choosing, where necessary, between competing versions of the way things were to be done (although, in so doing, they did not infrequently record minority opinions and traditions other than the one they ultimately upheld). This is where our traditional interpretations come from and why they were necessary.

JL: Yes, but that is to give a practical answer to a theoretical problem. Perhaps they did have to have unanimity. But still, here we have a Torah, whose authority comes from God, and then a body of interpretations passed on by human beings, people not very different from you and me. What's to stop me from coming along and interpreting the same text differently—and who's to say they're right and I'm wrong?

AA: To begin with, the Torah itself. For of course the problem of differing interpretations and applications of principle is one that is envisaged in the Torah, and its instructions are clear: in cases of dispute one must go to the human authorities, "to the levitical priests and to the judge that will be in that time." In other words, interpretation was not up to the individual but to the community and its established leadership. I would say that if this idea is difficult for you, it is that your own particular environment has conditioned you against it.

JL: How so?

AA: Just that America is a Protestant country, and Protestantism as a movement began as an attempt to overthrow the authority of a Church that claimed exclusive rights in interpreting Scripture. As a result, Protestants generally—indeed, Americans of all persuasions—seem to accept it as the normal state of affairs that the written text of the Bible alone is authoritative and that each little sect, perhaps even each individual, ought to go about trying to interpret its words according to his own abilities. But this never was the Jewish point of view. One might say that we have two fundamental sources of authority in Judaism, the written text and the traditions of our ancestors—or, as you now know them, the *torah she-bikhtav* and the *torah she-be'al peh,* the written and oral Torahs. But since the latter, those "traditions of our ancestors," are in large measure traditions about what the written text means, the two sources of authority are really inseparably one Torah. The very idea of Torah, in other words, consists of the words of the text as they have been interpreted and passed along in our traditions.

And I should add that the difference between written text and oral tradition is perhaps not so sharp as it might seem at first. For although our oral Torah was passed on from generation to generation by word of mouth, still there are more than a few written indications of these oral traditions even within the Bible, especially among the later books.

To take only the matter that you mentioned, how to keep Shabbat: if we looked in the Torah alone we would find only the general prohibition of work and the general injunction to keep Shabbat holy, as well as a few specifics, such as not to kindle fires or not to go out from one's "place" or to gather things like sticks or manna on the Sabbath. But in the book of Jeremiah it mentions specifically that Jews are not to "carry a burden from your houses" on Shabbat (down to, presumably, even the house key you mentioned), and elsewhere, in the book of Nehemiah, it speaks specifically of the prohibition of buying and selling on the Sabbath (whence, for example, the interdiction of even touching money). You might say that these things were implicit in the written Torah–but the fact that they surface in later books indicates that as the Torah was being passed on from generation to generation, so were these specifications and traditions about its meaning. And here is the point: for us these traditions have the same authority as the text, indeed, they are quite inseparable from it.

JL: Yes, but let us just suppose that someone were to come along nowadays and show that the original meaning of this or that word in the Torah is not as it has been generally interpreted–surely you encountered this in biblical criticism, didn't you?

AA: You still enthrone text above, and separate from, our traditional interpretations. Please understand that it is not stubbornness that makes me say what I am saying, but a fundamental conception in Judaism: the two are not separate. Torah for us is not simply the dry words of the text, but those words as they have been interpreted and applied from generation to generation. The things written by modern archaeologists and linguists and so forth can be very interesting, but their point of departure is quite different from ours. They imagine a text being uttered and then, as it were, frozen for all time, only to be defrosted now and examined in the light of modern knowledge of the ancient past. We, on the other hand, know this not to be the case. We did not just get the Torah yesterday, and it was never "frozen"–we have always had it, it was living among us at the time when Jeremiah prophesied and among us when Nehemiah led the people. And this *is* our Torah, the Torah that has been passed on and illuminated by our prophets and sages and augmented by the teachings and traditions of our people. It says in one part of the Bible that the words of Torah are like *masmerot netu'im,* "nails well planted." By this is meant that they do not move about but are fixed for all time. Yet our Rabbis characteristically, and perhaps representatively, gave the phrase a new twist and said that while words of Torah are indeed like *masmerot,* nails, they are also like *neta'im* or *neti'ot,* "plants," for like plants Torah is alive and vigorous, not dead. It lives among us as we live, and in fact, our Rabbis said, like a plant it also grows. By this they meant precisely that although the written text is fixed and finite, it has been accompanied by an oral tradition from earliest times, and the understanding and application of the written text has through this tradition continued to expand.

JL: Hm.

AA: What is it?

JL: Maybe it's just, as you say, the result of this Protestant environment. But it seems to me – in spite, incidentally, of what certain literary critics are saying nowadays – that a tradition of interpretation has to be somehow less than the text itself.

AA: Well, then, let me give you an American answer to your dilemma. In Aleppo I would simply have to say that these are our traditions, and that would be enough. For in Aleppo, if things have always been done or understood one way, who would even want to change, not to speak of daring to change? But in America perhaps it is better to put it this way: what is Torah for? A way of life, a way of serving God. And the traditions that we have for understanding Torah are inseparable from this way of life and always have been. Isn't one of the mottos of American industry, "If it isn't broken, don't fix it"? So let it be for Jews in America: our traditions are what constitute the way of Torah, and it is they that make it the basis of our lives and hearts.

JL: Both your Aleppo and your American answers seem to skirt the main issue, which is: what is the truth? What if I can show you that my explanation—based on archaeology or Old Babylonian or just common sense—is simply more likely, or more logical, than the one that was passed on by the Rabbis?

AA: You still do not grasp it. But your question recalls the famous tale in the Talmud of Rabbi Eliezer and the ringed oven—do you know it?

JL: No.

AA: Well. It seems that our Rabbis were at one point engaged in great debate over a certain sort of oven and its status vis-à-vis our laws of purity (these laws, incidentally, can be extremely complicated and intellectually challenging). Rabbi Eliezer, who was a great scholar, declared the particular form of oven in question to be acceptable from the standpoint of purity, but all the others declared it unacceptable. The principle in such disputes is that the majority view is adopted—indeed, there is a verse in our Torah itself on which this principle is based. But Eliezer nevertheless argued vigorously for his point of view, offering far more numerous and persuasive arguments than all his opponents. Finally, frustrated that he could not budge the majority, he cried out, "If the *halakhah* is indeed as I say, let this carob tree so demonstrate." Immediately, so the story goes, the tree was miraculously uprooted from the ground and traveled through the air quite some distance away. But this demonstration still did not affect the majority. Then Eliezer said, "If the *halakhah* is as I say, let this stream prove it." The stream at once began flowing backward. And so on with yet a further demonstration involving the walls of the study-house; but the Rabbis still remained unconvinced. Finally, a Heavenly voice called from above, "Why do you dispute with Rabbi Eliezer, since in all matters the *halakhah* is as he says?" Whereupon Rabbi Yehoshua retorted with a verse from the Torah itself: "It [i.e., the Torah] is not in Heaven." By this he meant to indicate that the Torah, once given from Heaven, was now in the hands of our sages and our traditions.

JL: What happened then?

156

AA: What happened? The majority ruled, that is what. In fact, our account in the Talmud goes on to record that the prophet Elijah later revealed himself to Rabbi Nathan, and the latter asked him what, as it were, was the reaction in Heaven to these events. Whereupon Elijah said that God had said, "My sons have defeated me." You see, the story is really a lesson about the authority of our Rabbis. The traditions they inherited and the things they further defined and decided constitute our oral Torah. The verse cited by Rabbi Yehoshua, "It is not in Heaven," is quite telling and contrasts well with the idea with which we began, *torah min ha-shamayim.* For if Torah is originally of divine origin, and as such has potentially unlimited meanings, it was nonetheless given to our people to be observed, and for this its meaning had to be clarified, and then its interpretation handed down and augmented by our sages in each age. So "The Torah is not in Heaven" is really a statement about what our oral traditions have done to the written text: its meaning is no longer "up in the air," so to speak.

The Bird's Nest

JL: In other words, the majority rule of the Rabbis can overcome the true interpretation—even if that interpretation is backed up by miracles and so forth.

AA: But it seems that we have changed sides here! A while ago you were speaking out against there being just *one* interpretation, the "true" one. Yet now you are disturbed that that "true" one did not win out in this particular case.

JL: I'm not disturbed. In fact, I think it seems okay, put in those terms. But still I'd like to come back to what we were talking about before—the ideas that are fundamental to Judaism. What about the view of how God acts in the world, reward and punishment, and so forth?

AA: Yes?

JL: I don't know. . . . Wouldn't you say that it's hard nowadays to conceive of things in such terms?

AA: I would say that it has always been hard. In fact, it would not be difficult to demonstrate that this was true of Judaism in the time of the Talmud, or even in the period of the Bible, for that matter. And yet there is a reason why we nonetheless hold to this belief: it is simply that, in the end, we do not seek to make God over in keeping with our understanding of the external world, but to shape our understanding of the world in keeping with God. This orientation is fundamental.

JL: Why do you say it was hard in the days of the Talmud?

AA: The evidence is there before us. Take the matter that you mentioned earlier, that of reward and punishment. It certainly would be correct to say that our Rabbis held that good deeds are ultimately rewarded and evil is punished. Yet they also believed that the processes of reward and punishment are not open to human inspection. They were fond of pointing out, for example, that the reward to be given for observance of this or that *mitzvah* in the Torah is rarely specified: we are generally told to serve God and keep the *mitzvot* simply because this is what is required, or because the *mitzvot* are our very life. And when a reward is spoken of in the Torah, our Rabbis sometimes understood it only as an indication of the uncanniness of the concept itself, in keeping with the verse, "How great is the goodness of Yours that You have *hidden aside* for those who fear You" (that is, it is hidden from ordinary contemplation). For example, the Torah specifies the same reward, "length of days," for two quite different *mitzvot,* that of honoring one's father and mother, and the *mitzvah* of *shilluaḥ ha-ken.*

JL: I don't know the second one.

AA: The Torah says that if one happens upon a bird's nest along one's way, one may not simply take the eggs or chicks and the mother bird sitting along with them, but that the mother bird must be set free. To our Rabbis this appeared not only as an outstanding example of God's mercy for all His creatures, but also as an illustration of the fact that our reward for keeping the *mitzvot* does not correspond to any pattern that humans might devise. After all, what could be easier to keep than this *mitzvah?* And on the other hand, is there a *mitzvah* more potentially difficult than honoring one's father and mother, which not only can involve considerable personal sacrifice—supporting them, for example, in their old age—but can easily lead one into positions and situations in which one's own beliefs or desires must be stifled or set aside? Yet, as I mentioned, precisely the same reward is specified for these two *mitzvot.* It is as if to say: who can fathom the reward for good?

159

JL: I see. What you're saying, in other words, is that the Judaism is basically noncommittal about reward and punishment.

AA: No, not that, certainly not. In fact, not only did the Rabbis believe in divine reward and punishment, they even believed that God's concern for justice in this regard was evident elsewhere in the same Torah, not the least in the Torah's apparent desire to "make the punishment fit the crime." As they expressed this principle: "In the measure that a person dishes out, so is it returned to him." And they lost no opportunity to point out examples in Scripture of what looked like an appropriate punishment. So, for example, Absolom, who was vain about his long locks, ultimately got caught by them in some low-hanging branches as he sought to escape his pursuers. On the other hand, the reward for good deeds is sometimes all out of proportion with the effort actually expended: Miriam waited only a few moments to see what would become of her brother Moses, but in recompense it later happened that the entire Israelite camp waited seven days for her in the desert when she was afflicted.

Yet certainly the Rabbis were likewise aware of the injustices of this world. In fact, they posed this question in terms of the very two *mitzvot* I mentioned before. What can one say, they asked, of a hypothetical son ordered by his father to fetch some pigeons from the roof? In observance of the aforementioned commandment, he took only the young pigeons and let the mother go, thus meriting twice over—because of having observed both the *mitzvah* of honoring his father, by doing his bidding, and the *mitzvah* of *shilluah ha-ken*—the reward of "length of days." Yet if it happened that on the way back down, the ladder gave way and he fell and died—"Where is his 'length of days'?" No doubt behind this theoretical question stands the bitter experience of more than one generation, of injustices that could not be banished from memory. Nevertheless, the Rabbis sought to affirm that justice ultimately is served and that goodness is rewarded, if not in this world then in the world to come.

JL: I'm not sure that we live in the very best century for the promulgation of such a doctrine.

160

AA: What do you mean?

JL: Well, after all, the Holocaust is still a recent memory – millions of people cruelly murdered, little children, some barely able to walk, sent to their deaths by the thousands. . . . Certainly some people have said that any doctrine of divine justice should hide its face in front of such a spectacle.

AA: I am sure it must seem so. And yet, as I wished to indicate before, it did not require the events of World War II to bring Jews to question the justice of this world. Indeed, if you think back to the Rabbis' own time, the world must have sometimes appeared to them too as a place directed in defiance of God's will. *Their* recent memory was not of the Holocaust but of the fall of Jerusalem to the Romans and, along with it, the destruction of the Temple. Now, not only did these events involve many deaths and personal tragedies (though, I will certainly warrant, not on the scale of World War II), but they also entailed the desecration of God's own house, the most sacred spot on earth. And if that were not enough, subsequent decades witnessed not only the death but the cruel execution, amid tortures, of the people's greatest sages and scholars, champions of Torah and of the *mitzvot*. Why these in particular? How could God abide their deaths, and the destruction of His Temple too, indeed, the cessation of the very service that He had ordained?

JL: And what's the answer?

AA: What should the answer be? Only that we are human beings and not God. It is not a small thing to turn one's thoughts to God. But if we do so, in the end we must do so all the way. Because, as I said, we shape our understanding of the world in keeping with God and not vice versa. In some premodern societies ordinary infant mortality can be as high as fifty percent; whole tribes or even nations are still being decimated by famine or by disease, and if you were to see with your own eyes the reality that lies behind such easy statements, believe me, you would wish to put your head in your hands and weep for the suffering. "Oh that my head were turned to water, and my eyes to a fountain of tears." Our Rabbis saw no less, and their eyes also wept tears. And certainly it must have been a temptation to maintain, as other peoples did, that there simply was no divine justice, that the world had been abandoned by its Creator to the designs of its most fiendish inhabitants, or even to deny as a category the power of God in the things of this world. Still they did not do so but strove to believe, to proclaim, that God's justice will triumph. And so must anyone do whose heart is truly turned to God. It is an easy thing to worship God in the midst of prosperity, but our way is to worship Him as well in adversity.

JL: I know that. It is just hard to put it together with the reality of what has happened.

AA: There is a verse that well expresses where the love of God may sometimes lead us. It says, "Come let us turn to God, for He who has maimed will also heal us, He who strikes down binds up our wounds." Our whole posture toward God—*katonti,* as I have said—must in the end dictate that we accept. I do not say this glibly, nor with any satisfaction. But God is God and we are only human beings, and there is no matter in which this is either clearer or more difficult to accept than the one you mention.

JL: But apart from that, it seems to me, there is the matter of the Jews in particular. Certainly anyone who surveys human history for the last two millennia would notice that the one people singled out for suffering is precisely that people that conceives of itself as chosen by God.

History

AA: But Judd—this is why I say that you must plunge yourself into everything concerning Judaism. I know that it is the practice of some people, indeed, even of some Jews, to view our history as one unremitting series of catastrophes—but you must know by now that this is just not true. In fact, it is a perversion of the truth, and one that springs from a kind of arrogance. For just as Christians have at times exaggerated Jewish suffering in order to "prove" that we have been punished for the alleged crime of "deicide," so some Jews have sought to exaggerate our misfortunes in order to stress our uniqueness as a people or our heroic endurance of martyrdom. In so doing, however, they make us out to be an *'am medushenei 'onesh,* a people sated with punishment, which is, as I say, a perversion. Given the basic geopolitical facts of most of our history—the fact that, even in our homeland, we sat at the crossroads of empires, and the fact that, for most of the last two millennia, we have been excluded from that homeland, a people of exiles ——

JL: That's a lot to "give". . . .

AA: Perhaps, but the former seems to be practically a natural feature of the landscape, mere geography, and the latter is in some sense only a consequence of the former, specifically, a consequence of the Roman conquest of this crucial piece of territory in the first century. In any case, what I was going to say was that, during those years of exile, we have fared rather well, by and large. There have been, of course, terrible tragedies, outright persecutions and expulsions, the Crusades, the expulsion from Spain in 1492, pogroms in Poland and

Russia, and, of course, the latest and most devastating tragedy. But against these one must weigh years of relative tranquillity and even prosperity in dozens of different lands, centuries through which we were able to maintain the delicate balance of remaining a people-within-a-people (and not infrequently a state-within-a-state) while at the same time living side by side with non-Jewish neighbors and yet largely avoiding friction. No easy task—to be Jews and be recognized as such, yet not to be perceived as such outsiders that the jealousy or simple xenophobia of the non-Jews might spill over into violence or persecution. I daresay there have been other peoples in history who have fared far worse, some wholly slipping off in either of the directions named—that is, they have either been annihilated by the wrath of their neighbors or assimilated and swallowed up by their acceptance.

JL: I see.

AA: And through it all, I must say (without in any way attributing this fact to our political or material circumstances, which I think would be mistaken) we have, as a people, managed to create extraordinary collective and individual achievements. Certainly (though perhaps we ought not to take credit for this) the Jewish understanding of things, our adherence to God and to Torah, has shaped the thinking of the world. This everyone recognizes. For however much Islam and Christianity may have gone off in their own directions, it is nonetheless true that at bottom their belief in a single divine will—and the understanding of the world that derives from it, their ideas of morality and justice and answerability to God—came from Judaism, as did, in much more concrete terms, a good bit of their religious and legal practices, their Scripture and form of worship. But leave the matter of influence aside; consider only what the Jewish people themselves have done. The absence of political sovereignty, although it certainly has not made collective action or even individual achievement easier for us, has nonetheless not ruled out either of these. It was in exile in Babylon, as well as in a Palestine ruled by outsiders, that the great corpus of our rabbinic writings was put together, with the extraordinary subtlety of thought that characterizes our legal writings and the

164

poetic creativity of our *aggadah*. This is not to mention the prayers and synagogue poems that were composed at that time, a vast literature that in more than one way puts to shame the efforts of other peoples of the same period, who, however, enjoyed the support and wealth of nations. Then travel to Rome, or a bit later to Spain, where Jews not only further developed these same pursuits, but entered new ones—again, this is a time of extraordinary literary creativity in all genres: poetry, secular as well as religious, and also philosophy, Kabbalah, philology, astronomy, and so forth. For a while, Spain was also a place where Jews rose to positions of real political prominence, more than one of them assuming, as had our ancestor Joseph, the reins of an entire Gentile state; and thinkers like Maimonides or ibn Gabirol, while of course extraordinarily important to our own tradition, likewise exercised no small influence on the thinking of non-Jewish philosophers and theologians. Meanwhile, in France there was Rashi and his school of Talmudists, and not long afterward, the rise of new centers of Jewish learning in Italy and elsewhere. And so has it been since then, in Germany, in Poland and Lithuania, in North Africa and Turkey and Iraq and elsewhere—save that, in modern times, Jews have once again branched out into fields of endeavor that had for centuries been closed to them in one or another locale, and they have prospered all out of proportion to their numbers. Look at this country— one scarcely knows where to begin! In business, in science, medicine, the arts, entertainment, education—there is no area that I can think of where a Jewish name does not spring to the lips as one of the outstanding practitioners, if not *the* outstanding one, and there are a few areas where one would be hard pressed to cite a non-Jew! Indeed, many non-Jews, if you were to ask them—in consideration of these facts—to guess what percentage of the world's population we constitute, would surely come up with a figure such as fifteen, or at least ten, percent. Yet even an answer of one percent would be many times too high. For we are only a tiny band among the races of men, and so it always has been. Even in the Torah it says, "Not because you are more numerous than other peoples did God take pleasure in you; for you are indeed the smallest of peoples." Perhaps it all sounds like boasting, but this little census, which has not troubled to, but could, get down to naming the actual Freuds and Einsteins in each country and each field, should be sufficient to give the lie to the notion that we are a people distinguished principally by our suffering.

JL: I suppose you're right. In any case, certainly now Jews seem to be doing all right in most parts of the world. And if the cause of past suffering was the absence of a country of our own – well, I guess that's changed now too. Although that's something else that's been on my mind, Israel.

Israel

AA: Well, again, I am sure that you can find out much more on this topic from other sources. All I wished to do was to get you started in Judaism, and that—I hope, anyway—has been done as well as it could be, under the circumstances.

JL: Yes, but certainly the existence of Israel has something to do with Judaism, doesn't it? Isn't it, in fact, considered a *mitzvah* to settle in the land of Israel? Though I guess you must not think so, or else you wouldn't be in New York.

AA: If you are asking a question of *halakhah,* I can tell you simply that there are different opinions on this subject. And, of course, the issue of living in Eretz Yisrael is entwined, but not coextensive, with the rise of the modern state of Israel as a politically sovereign entity. As you may know, there are even some Jews (though they are not many) who refuse to recognize the legitimacy of this Israeli sovereignty and continue to wait for some more clearly Heaven-sent event before returning there. None of this, however, has anything to do with my presence in New York.

JL: No?

AA: Perhaps some day we may talk about it. But do you know that I did live for some years in Jerusalem? Yes, and I do hope to go back there before too long. For me it is practically the land of my birth, and when I am there, in the white, white glare of the morning sun—so bright you almost have to squint as you look about the city—or when

I walk along dusty roads, with that whiteness, and the old stone houses, and even the particular shade of the dust, lighter and yellower than here, not as gray—well, of course, it reminds me very much of Aleppo, the sights and smells, the gardens . . . and so I feel very much at home. For Americans, of course, things are different—the ones that go to live in Israel usually do so at the cost of some personal dislocation, as well as material sacrifice.

JL: I take it it's generally a matter of people who are religious, though.

AA: Well, this is yet another of history's ironies. I suppose Zionism represents, in a certain sense, nothing less than the age-old dream of the Jewish people. But must you really lead me into this topic? Well, then. Throughout the centuries of exile we have prayed—you must know this, since it is part of the *Amidah* itself—for the gathering of all Jews back to our land and, with it, the reestablishment of our country's fortunes as they once were, and the return of the House of David to the throne of Israel. Indeed, it is our well-known tradition that the *mashiah*—this Hebrew word, which means simply "anointed [king]," long ago entered English in the form "messiah"—will arise from among David's descendants and will personally inaugurate the new age.

Yet if Zionism, in that sense, represents the embodiment of our tradition, its actual political origins were somewhat different. It is a movement that essentially began in the latter part of the nineteenth century (though it did have some forerunners a bit earlier) and was animated principally by the geopolitical facts of the time and by the peculiar, and somewhat precarious, position of large segments of European Jewry in the wake of Emancipation (as we have discussed). Zionism came to pose itself to European Jewry as the solution to the "Jewish Question" (as the situation of our people was at times called). For Theodor Herzl, in some respects the founder of modern Zionism, the prospect of a Jewish homeland represented the best solution to the anti-Semitism he found endemic not only in his native Austria but throughout the supposedly enlightened capitals of Europe. The New Zion, for Herzl, was thus principally to be a refuge from anti-Semitism. It was certainly not a necessity for all Jews to go there, but (as he pointed out in a famous simile) the flame of anti-Semitism would keep the Zionist pot bubbling and ensure a steady stream of immigrants to the proposed Jewish state. But these details must strike one as a bit ironic nowdays.

JL: How so?

AA: Because everything seems to be rather the opposite just now. If anti-Semitism is still about in the world, certainly one of its principal targets seems to be the state of Israel itself. In that sense I suppose the chances for physical survival, in raw percentages, look better for a Jew outside of Israel than for an Israeli, what with the necessity the latter faces for lifelong military service, plus the danger posed to Israeli civilians by individual acts of terror or (Heaven forbid) even worse at the hands of Israel's enemies.

JL: What about the question of religion and Zionism?

AA: Quite so. Herzl, as you know, was a secularist, quite ignorant, in fact, of Judaism; and the state that he envisaged was likewise a secular, pluralistic state. A similar vision animated those who actually went on to settle in Palestine—though here I should perhaps note that, despite our dispersion, there had almost always been a sizable Jewish contingent in Jerusalem or environs—in that very limited sense, in any case, it had never ceased being our homeland. And if I use the name "Palestine," by the way, it is only because this land was so known to the world from the time of our exile—not by our choice, but by that of the Romans, who hoped that in changing its name they might obliterate our people's age-old connection to this territory.

JL: I didn't know that.

AA: Yes. But despite the origins of this name, Jews in the period in question—the late nineteenth and early twentieth centuries—sometimes adopted it proudly: they spoke of the "rebirth of Palestine," and even of themselves as "Palestinians." In any case, what I wished to say was that these settlers, particularly the later groups, also were by and large moved by a secular vision (though perhaps not quite so secular as they themselves imagined). Their political philosophy was socialism, and in founding a homeland for the Jewish people they also hoped to build a nation scientifically organized on socialist principles, communal ownership and so forth. And they were, for the most part, quite estranged from traditional Jewish practice—so much so that there were not inconsiderable conflicts between them and the (traditionally religious) Jewish communities of Jerusalem and other centers. So here is another tricky turn taken by history that would quite confound Herzl and his followers. For despite their vision, despite even the largely secular character of the state that was finally established in 1948, Israel has not ceased to become more and more concerned with religious issues; indeed, much of its domestic politics now turns on conflicts between secularist and religious factions, with the latter ever more powerful. And, in terms of immigration, it is not only anti-Semitism that has kept the Zionist pot bubbling these days, but Judaism—for many new immigrants to Israel, especially from the West, have gone there out of frankly religious reasons.

JL: So where does all this leave modern Israel vis-à-vis traditional Jewish beliefs?

AA: As I said, there are some religious Jews who hold that, in the absence of a clear sign from Heaven, indeed, a *mashiah* with all the traditional trappings, Zionism is to be viewed as nought but a human initiative, indeed, a bit of hubris that cannot but bring down punishment on all who espouse it. There are, believe it or not, Jews who hold to this philosophy even as they live in Jerusalem, protected by the Jewish state they abhor.

JL: So I hear.

AA: On the other hand, the position of *most* religious Jews (as well as secularists, for that matter) is that the state of Israel is an overwhelmingly good thing and may indeed herald, as the rabbinate of that state has delicately put it, "the beginning of our redemption's flourishing." And certainly it has already brought about an unprecedented Jewish revival. The Hebrew language was never quite dead—it

170

was always understood by ordinary Jews and was the language of religious and even secular writing and higher studies for educated Jews for many a century. But look at it today—it has passed from being a book language to being the natural idiom of a whole, bustling civilization: this was no mean feat to accomplish in a generation or two! And with it has come the rebirth of everything Jewish—Jewish literature, philosophy, the university study of Judaism in all its facets, not to speak of the proliferation of traditional Jewish institutions, schools and yeshivot. And here I am thinking not only of what goes on in Israel, but of just these things as they have developed in America—for I am mindful, in a way that most American Jews are not, I suspect, of just how much Judaism and Jewish institutions in this country owe their vigor (such as it may be) to the existence of a Jewish state beyond the sea. In all these respects I think the creation of Israel must be viewed by Jews as an overwhelmingly good thing, and this despite the many tragedies and sacrifices along the way, the hundreds and thousands of lives that have been snuffed out in the attainment of this dream.

JL: But that does bring up another side of the question. The sacrifices have not been exclusively Jewish ones, and I notice that your account makes scarce mention even of the existence of the Palestinian Arabs. Isn't it true that the dream of Jewish nationalism has been realized only at the cost of crushing an equally valid national movement, and one with an equally valid claim to the same piece of territory?

AA: I certainly share your sympathy for the Palestinian Arabs, if not your diagnosis of the cause of their sufferings. For no one but a brute could feel any satisfaction at what has happened to them. Still, your version of things—which seems to be quite common in America nowadays—is not one that I myself can endorse. It is hardly a situation of two competing nationalisms and two equally valid claims.

JL: No?

AA: I do not know what it is that entitles any people to claim a particular connection or right to a piece of the surface of this earth, but

171

I do believe that it all resides in the world of ideas rather than biology. That is, I do not think that there is in anyone a physiological basis for his claim to belonging to this or that land, or this or that land's belonging to him. And so he bases that attachment on other things: he belongs there because he was born there or grew up there; he belongs there because he has purchased that piece of territory according to the laws of the land, and it is his; he belongs there—perhaps this is the most common to spring to mind—because he is a part of such-and-such a people, and this is their homeland (which is only to project these same arguments from the level of a single individual to that of a group). And so forth. I am not sure how one is to choose among these reasons or to compare one with another; but what I wish to say, first of all, is that in the end they all strike me as collectively rather flimsy. We Jews believe that our claim to the land is ultimately rooted in God's choice, and yet, in the Torah, even this connection—which (you will imagine) I like better—is conditional on our adherence to the *mitzvot*. And more than once that connection's precariousness is highlighted: the land truly belongs only to God, making us, in the Torah's pungent phrase, mere "squatters and sojourners with Me."

But to return: whatever the basis for a people's claim to the land, I believe that there is no comparing that of the Jews to that of the Arabs in this case—not, of course, that acceptance of this fact makes the political problem any easier; but it is nevertheless something that ought to be said. Surely no one ought to dare compare the Palestinian cause, aimed principally at relieving their people from statelessness and powerlessness, both in part imposed upon them by their fellow Arabs—no one dare compare this local political claim, however strongly made, to the fervent attachment of two millennia and the sacrifices that have accompanied it, the drumbeat of "Jerusalem, Jerusalem" that has been the unceasing pulse of Jewish hopes for twenty centuries, as well as the still-remembered struggle to realize those hopes not in warfare and terrorist bombs, but in malaria-ridden swamps, in arid wastes, that now are nothing less than the food supply of a nation, collective farms and farming settlements that are no abstract testimony to a people's attachment to a particular place. I do not say that the Palestinian Arabs might not show a similar dedication over two millennia of exile and a similar devotion in realizing their dreams – but the one is historical fact, the other wishful hypothesis. How dare the two be compared?

JL: But that's still sort of irrelevant now.

AA: Perhaps – but if that is irrelevant, then what is relevant? As I say, ultimately, there is no mark on a person's body that will vouchsafe his belonging to a piece of land. So if it is not the tangible proof of his dedication, then what is it? If purchase is what gives one title, the Jews have purchased – starting in the nineteenth century and going on almost until the time of the state itself. If it is by blood that one wins title, then the Jews have won on that dubious score as well. If it is only by military might and Realpolitik – well, here too the facts speak for themselves. If it is birth or upbringing, well, these are in truth but the children of Realpolitik, but the fact is that today most of the Jewish population of Israel is native-born, whereas many "Palestinians" have never seen Palestine. I do not say this gleefully, but it is nevertheless a fact.

JL: But I'm afraid that none of your "facts" make the life of the Palestinians any easier, or hold out any more obvious political solution.

AA: Quite so. I only wished to take issue with your characterization of the nature of the claims involved. Indeed, I have not quite finished. For even the "two competing nationalisms" analysis is one I must take issue with, though this is perhaps the most vexed part of all. It is true that to an American, things are no doubt quite obvious: every people is a people, and every people has a homeland, or should. And yet I beg you to put on my Aleppo spectacles, which are, after all, native to that region. Then you would see that things are hardly so clear. Nationalism as such is a European idea, imported late and only imperfectly to the Middle East. For centuries inhabitants of that region had thought of themselves – in fact, still do – not principally as Saudis or Jordanians – these are, in some cases, little more than passport designations – but as Arabs or as Moslems. As I say, you may find this difficult to believe, but it may be easier if you compare it to the situation in the United States itself just now: for to what extent do people here think of themselves as Iowans or Massachusettsans (or whatever the proper form may be)? I think in most cases only to a rather limited degree—they are principally Americans, Americans who happen this year to live in Boston or San Francisco, but whose identity would not be radically shaken if, next year, they undertook even a transcontinental shift; for they are fundamentally only Americans. The analogy is imperfect, since in the Middle East people are, to begin with, rather radically more attached to place than here: but that place is Aleppo or Damascus, not Syria—indeed, an Aleppan considers Damascus virtually as much of a foreign city as Beirut or Baghdad. And on the other hand, the supranational entities—*al-'Arabiyya, al-Islam*—have a reality in people's thinking, in the press, on radio, in political speeches, for which it is hard even to find an American analogue. This reality is rooted in many things, most significantly, the political movements of the last century in the Arab world. But I am sure if you knew it for what it is, if you could live, in fact, in the Arab world for a time, you would come to see that the very idea of nation states there is not what it is here. And perhaps the most striking proof of this are the ever-renewed efforts to form some supranational political union of existing states, something that would somehow reconcile Western-style nationalism with the people's own sense that *al-'Arabiyya* is one entity, or ought to be.

JL: I'm not sure I get the drift of what you are saying.

AA: Only that, from within this mentality, there was no particular logic to a Palestinian state for the Palestinian people—the latter really is a creation of the conflict between Israel and its neighbors. Had those neighbors absorbed the Arab refugees instead of sticking them into refugee camps, I daresay there would be no Palestinian exiles but simply Jordanians, Syrians, Lebanese, etc. I am not saying that they would not have suffered from the wars any less (though, of course, their material situation and physical lot in life would in some cases be much improved if they could live as citizens in the lands of their dispersion); but I am saying that something less than *identity*, the right to be what one is, is really involved. In this respect, too, there is an asymmetry between the Jewish and Arab claims.

JL: But I'm afraid it all trails off into the familiar claims and counter-claims.

AA: Perhaps so. In any case, if I have followed you into this topic, it is because Israel—and for that matter, the issue of the Jewish suffering in World War II that you mentioned—do in their own way have more than a little to do with what we were discussing before, being a Jew in America. For it has often occurred to me that the fact of the Holocaust and the existence of the state of Israel together may have more to do with the undoing of Judaism in this country than even the existence of American Jewry's various factions.

JL: What do you mean?

Elsewhere

AA: Just that for a great many American Jews nowadays, even those who are somehow involved in Jewish communal affairs or perhaps synagogues, these two things, Israel and the Holocaust, are the twin foci of what it means for them to be Jews.

JL: What's wrong with that?

AA: It is not only that (in regard to the Holocaust) suffering, or death, is hardly an inspiring banner to hold up to the next genera-tion—nor, as I said, is suffering in any case the true significance or even leitmotiv of Jewish history. But beyond such distortions, it is true that these twin principles, the Holocaust and Israel, in fact have something in common with each other: they are both, conveniently perhaps, elsewhere. And so American Judaism in general has an "else-where" quality to it: it is "there," in Israel or back in the Old Country, that Jews could be said to be really Jews, and it is "there" that the sig-nificant Jewish events of our age have happened or are happening. Such reality as American Judaism might have is therefore wholly derivative, a kind of Judaism once removed. I am not even thinking of the Holocaustolatry that in fact afflicts many a comfortable subur-ban congregation, whose purpose sometimes seems to be to turn this tragedy into a series of ready-made experiences for the next genera-tion, like macabre amusement park rides—"Holo-coasters," I call them. Nor yet do I speak of the "instant Old Country" that Israel has become for a whole segment of American Jewry: though they may in fact have never been there, Israel has become a kind of surrogate point of origin for them, spoken of with the same rapt sentimentality that

Italo-Americans reserve for Calabria or Irish Americans for County Cork. But even putting aside these silly excesses, it seems to me that this elsewhere quality of American Judaism is right now its greatest affliction.

JL: But isn't it a natural consequence of what you are always talking about, the fact that Judaism in this country is a relatively recent arrival? So, of course, it is still "elsewhere." And, on the other hand, if Israel really is the fulfillment of our age-old dream, isn't it appropriate that it utterly dominate, eclipse even, American Jews' own conception of themselves?

AA: Perhaps, Yehuda. But in raising these questions I was really thinking about you.

JL: What do you mean?

AA: My question is: what is to become of you? You see, you have come part of the way, and perhaps you will go further. But now I see that you may also slide, in a way that surely is not yet apparent to yourself, into a kind of Jewish elsewhereness of your own. I am a foreigner, you see, and no matter how long I live in New York it will always be that way. My roots *are* elsewhere, in an unrecoverable Aleppo and in Jewish communities that are, for me, equally scattered here and there, New York and Paris and Geneva and Jerusalem. I know that I am in exile. But you, on the other hand, are from here, and quite comfortable here, and precisely because American Judaism is what it is, I can see you settling into the halfway affair that Judaism is in this country, accompanied, as it is, by that relentless gesture of concession to the "elsewheres."

JL: That's not really fair. Halfway was where I was before. If all this talking has convinced me of one thing, it's —

AA: I hope so. But that is not what I was speaking of. You don't see what I mean? Perhaps, then, this is the way to put it: that just now, in America, I can think of no casual way for one to be a Jew, truly a Jew, no easy and natural Jewish existence such as has been found elsewhere in different communities throughout Jewish history. What is easy and natural here is halfway Jewish, the Jewish hobby or social affiliation, and that must finally prove a dead end.

JL: What solution is there?

AA: In general? I suppose time will resolve things one way or another. It may be, though I cannot quite see how, that being a Jew here will end up as it was in Aleppo and elsewhere, that there will be an American way of being Jewish that is wholly both, and therefore comfortable. But that is certainly far off, and in the meantime—what of you? I do sincerely hope that you find some way of your own to be a Jew here, fully a Jew. You at least know now most of what is involved. And remember that in the end it is always a matter of the heart. Do you follow me?

JL: Yes.

AA: Because right now it strikes me that the principal accomplishment of the "elsewhere" orientation of American Jewry is to make halfway, half-hearted Judaism the comfortable, and apparently natural, thing that it is here. And this is what I would hope you can somehow avoid. To be a Jew most earnestly here, and without reference to either of these "elsewheres," this is the thing—unless, in the case of Israel, it is eventually your intention to go there and settle, in which case, by all means, go. But in the meantime I hope that you will turn your heart wholly to our *halakhah* and—although this is hardly the aim—that in so doing you will not concede anything to the elsewheres but will earnestly set about the business of being wholly a Jew here and now. That is it. Perhaps this must eventually lead you to Israel—I do not know. But for now, not to be a Jew halfway. Yehuda, our course is at an end. *Ḥazak uvarukh, ḥazak ve-ematz.*

PART V

The time: some months later

Israelis

AA: Well, Judd, this is most unexpected.

JL: I would have called, but, frankly, I wanted to tell you the news in person. You see, I've decided to go to Israel.

AA: Really.

JL: Yes. My dissertation topic has been approved, and I think I can do the writing as well there as here, although it will mean a lot of long distance phone calls and special delivery envelopes. But, frankly, I'm just dying to go right now. Not only because I'm sure it will help my Hebrew, but because I'm anxious to see Jerusalem, of course, and get to know Israel and some Israelis. And just to go. I also hope that when I get there I'll be able to start studying in a yeshiva, at least part-time, while I'm writing.

AA: Hm.

JL: The more I've thought about it, the more I feel I just *have* to go, perhaps even for good. That's how I feel now, anyway; anything else would be a contradiction. My heart's in the East, yet here I am in the far-most West.

AA: I believe I have heard that someplace before. . . .

JL: Oh?

AA: No matter. Well, I'm very happy for you, Yehuda, and I certainly hope it all works out for the best.

JL: Somehow it doesn't sound like you think it will.

AA: Oh no, I'm sure you'll manage fine. It's just that I wish we had had some more time, I really would have liked to prepare you for this step.

JL: How do you mean?

AA: Well, you know, there are many people I know in Jerusalem, and yeshivot. . . .

JL: You can still give me the names now.

AA: Also, frankly, I would have liked to prepare you to . . . to get you over some of the rough spots.

JL: Rough spots?

AA: Yes. The fact is, I know many Americans, some your age and some older, who have left for Israel with precisely the same fervent enthusiasm that you now show, and almost all of them have returned a year or two later, disappointed. I just wish I could spare you that.

JL: Disappointed?

AA: Yes. It didn't work out, Israel wasn't this, the people were too that. . . .

JL: Too what?

AA: It does not matter. The point is, you are going to a different country, a different culture—despite all the things that bind Jews together—and you must be prepared for a bit of an adjustment, I can tell you this from my own experience.

JL: But I thought you said that you felt at home there. Or did you leave because it just didn't correspond to what you had hoped for?

AA: No, not that. It was more that, when I lived there, my family's business, in which I had been trained, could not be transplanted, nor was there a ready alternative. There were also many hurdles to private investment then, so gradually I found myself spending more and more time abroad. Then too, in the fifties and even sixties the country was still very much run by Ashkenazim, the European Jews, who were largely secularists to boot. That is what I meant when I said I also had had a bit of an adjustment, I and my countrymen as well.

JL: Yes?

AA: This is, of course, not directly relevant to you, so perhaps I ought not to go on—but it also was the cause of some regret to me. For the fact is, the Jews who founded the state were by and large Russians and Poles, with a few Germans and Rumanians and the like. They had no feel for the sort of communities we had lived in (save, perhaps, for the few Sephardim they encountered in Jerusalem), and when we arrived in great numbers in the early 1950s from Iraq and North Africa and so forth, they regarded us not only as newcomers, but as backward, uneducated, boors. And, perhaps, in terms of Westernization, this was true of at least some. But we also came from very static, structured communities, each with its own rich traditions. To them our names meant nothing or seemed, at best, the Eastern equivalents of Rosenblatt and Greenberg, insignificant labels no doubt chosen for the convenience of Gentile tax-collectors. But to us our names—Harari, Zilkha, Kadouri, Abu-ḥazeira—were everything; they told not only where we came from, but who we were. And we *were* somebody, centuries of somebodies, yet they looked at us and saw only people in need of becoming more like themselves.

And then there was the matter of language. They wished to speak Hebrew, and yet somehow they were always surprised that we didn't know at least a *little* Yiddish—some are still surprised to this day. And the Hebrew they did speak—was this Hebrew? It was not the language of the Bible or the Mishnah, although its words seemed to come from there. But the whole sentence structure, the rhythm of the language, yes and even the meaning that was given to words taken from Bible and Mishnah, they were all quite unrecognizable. The same was true, flagrantly so, of the way this Hebrew was pronounced, with that Germanic, guttural *r* instead of a rolled one, and no distinction made between totally different sounds—*ḥet* and *khaf, aleph* and *'ayin, tet* and *tav,* and so forth. This too, I later discovered, was no accident, but simply the result of the transference to Hebrew of Yiddish phonology—modern Hebrew was to have no sound that did not already exist in Yiddish. And even this would not have been grievous were it not that they then had the audacity to make fun of *our* pronunciation! But no doubt I am too harsh.

JL: No, go on.

AA: No, I have finished. All these things are, in fact, more understandable in context. For this was a period of great stress in Israel, not only because of the external political threat, but precisely because the state was then confronted with the awesome task of accepting a whole new influx of immigrants, an overwhelmingly large influx, and most of them quite penniless, since their wealth had been confiscated as the price of an exit visa. It is certainly understandable that they might resent us, all the more so because, as newcomers, we had not suffered through the hardships of the prestate period or even the War of Independence. And faced with such a massive immigration and the potential upsets it presented, their reaction was to homogenize the population as best they could, seeking specifically to break up traditional communities and national groups, sending some here and some there, and trying to make us just "Israelis." But what they did not realize is that in so doing they were annihilating our differentness and trying to make us just like themselves. And I must say, in this they have basically succeeded. Oh, just now in Israel there is a lot of talk on the radio and television about "Sephardic culture" and the importance of the "Oriental heritage," but the truth is that most of that heritage has been eroded. Hebrew is still as it was before, but now our children speak it as well as theirs, and with the same dreadful accent. Our societies, like all those in the Middle East, stressed the virtues of respectfulness, modesty, and dignity—but it is hard to maintain these in an informal, bustling, and brash culture, and so they have been abandoned by a younger generation taught to regard its own parents as, in the best case, ineffectual and hopelessly outmoded. The only refuge for the parents—the only place where our names still meant something, and where our old ways still reigned unchallenged—was the synagogue, because here Sephardim and Ashkenazim observed a strict separation, each with its own services and places of worship. But, alas, now all our Sephardic *hakhamim* have been trained, directly or indirectly, by Ashkenazim, who for so long staffed and directed the schools and yeshivot.

JL: I guess I can see why some Sephardim might have wanted to leave.

AA: Can you? Yet just now, I confess, I myself regret leaving. For although these problems existed, the problems in America are, in the end, no less troubling, though material conditions are certainly better here. Indeed, I have found it a general rule that, while the disadvantages of Israel are easy enough to name, there are advantages to it that are quite intangible but nonetheless can seem overwhelming at times. And this is what I wanted to say, Judd. Don't be put off by the Israeli brashness or any of the other things. Don't even be put off by the fact that when (as you may) you announce to others there that you are considering remaining in Israel and becoming their countryman, many will, despite what they say in words, come to look at you askance; for they themselves often do not know what it means to live in Israel, although they live there. So if they ask you why you wish to stay, you must tell them it is because of the tomatoes.

JL: Tomatoes?

AA: They are very tasty there—not at all like the durable, tasteless variety that is sold in New York. The tomatoes there are fine, and the olives, and also the afternoon sun—not at all like here, where at times it can have a subtlety quite magnificent, this I concede—but there it is very, very bright, so much so that you must squint when you stand outside, and the sunlight in America seems simply dim and pale by comparison. Then the morning's whiteness turns later to a gold or copperish color that is smeared over everything; it is quite impressive. When you go there, Judd, I hope you will keep these things in mind and forget about all the rest.

JL: But the Jewish people, the Jewish state. . . .

AA: Quite so, quite so. And yet, in my experience, it is the Zionists who return to America and only the tomato lovers who stay. And I should want you to be able to stay, if you choose.

JL: Yes.

AA: And one more thing. I hope that when you are there, you will not forget that you are an American.

JL: That's a strange thing for you to say. You have not had too much good to say about America.

AA: Perhaps, yet I do not think that what I mean is inconsistent with what I have said before. For as I once explained, when I see you, I see more than Judd Lewis; I see generations and generations, going back to Europe and deep into European Jewish history, back to the same cities and towns inhabited by the ancestors of today's Israelis. At a certain point, not too long ago in fact, your ancestors chose to go to America, while theirs stayed put and later went to Palestine. Both decisions were largely a matter of pragmatism, and their descendants ought not to exalt themselves now for having been born in one place or another.

JL: I don't get your meaning.

AA: It is just that, despite a certain homogeneity in Israeli society just now, you should not feel pressured, as no doubt you will, to become more like them, as if that were somehow more legitimate; to be an American Jew is perfectly fine. And so please, speak Hebrew with your American *r*, and in a thousand other ways too, stick to what you are, even if it means bucking the tide.

JL: Yes.

AA: And so for the important things too, though about this I have no fear. You know what it is now, I think, to be a Jew: our *halakhah*, and the *mishkan* of the heart; what it means to walk in *kedushah*; what our prayers are, and Shabbat and our festivals; and what, most of all, it is for the heart to reach out to God-in-particular, "to love and serve Him with your whole heart and soul." These are the fixed points, and I hope each has a vivid meaning for you in your own heart.

JL: Yes.

186

AA: Good. Then I can only wish you success – perhaps over another glass of Araq? And I hope that, God willing, we will meet again soon, here or perhaps even there. But in the meantime, *leḥayyim.*

Afterword

In the course of teaching at a university for some years, I have on occasion been asked by a student—in a hesitant conversation after class, and only after some long preliminaries—a particular sort of question, which, however worded, came down to: What is it *like* to live according to the traditional Jewish way? And why should anyone nowadays willingly take on all the obligations of that way of life, the Sabbath and dietary laws and so forth? I remember these conversations in detail, and in particular the frustration that I felt in trying to formulate my answers. There are, of course, many books that explain how to observe Jewish laws and traditions, and others that set out the history of Judaism and its development; at first I tried to refer my students to such works as these. Later I came to recognize that their questions were of a more basic sort, and more personal. For my interlocutors, the issue now looming was similar to the one that "AA" describes in the preceding pages as "to Jew or not to Jew." For although my students had been born Jews, and some of them had even received some rudimentary Jewish education, they had not had until recently any real inkling of what it means to be a Jew, nor any sense of the traditional Jewish way of life and how it is followed in modernday America—no sense, for that matter, of why Judaism in America is what it is, or how it got that way. But now, having gained just an inkling, some few at least found themselves in the necessity of finding out more.

And so I resolved to try to put some sort of answer to their questions down on paper. In casting about for a model for a such a work, I soon thought of the classic *Book of the Kuzari* by the great medieval

Hebrew poet Yehudah ha-Levi. That book took the form of a series of imaginary conversations between a learned Jew and the king of the Kuzars (Khazars), an ancient people that lived not far from the Caspian Sea, as the king contemplated conversion to Judaism. This form—and specifically the putting of his protagonist in the position of having to explain things to someone to whom many aspects of Judaism might at first appear quite foreign—allowed ha-Levi to examine Judaism from a distance and so to treat some of the most basic issues connected to his subject. I could not hope, nor did I even wish, to imitate the *Kuzari's* masterly, detailed presentation of traditional Jewish learning; but I thought that its outward form—or rather, a "translation" of that form into modern America—might well serve my purpose. Indeed, it seemed to me that it would be both an appropriate and ironic reflection on the current state of American Jewry if I were to substitute for that book's Khazar convert someone who (like my students) already was a Jew, but one quite ignorant of traditional Jewish practice and belief—someone, in fact, only now considering "converting" to the religion that was his by birth. And it further occurred to me that my recasting would be still more pointed if I were to make that Jew none other than the American incarnation of the *Kuzari's* own erudite poet-author, here turned into a young poet-questioner taking his first steps on the path of Judaism. And so Yehudah ha-Levi became Judd Lewis, graduate student and aspiring American poet, a young man just now a bit interested, yet quite untutored, in the religion of his people. For his interlocutor I chose another sort of Jew entirely, an outsider not only vis-à-vis American Judaism but the European Judaism from which it is sprung, and thus someone able, in another sense, to see his subject from afar.

I will not apologize further for the too brief and schematic treatment of the various topics touched upon in this book, a failing only highlighted by any comparison of it to its literary model. But I would point out that the two books were written for two very different audiences. Yehudah ha-Levi's explanations were addressed to the Khazar king only as a literary fiction; his real addressee was his own educated Jewish contemporary, who might find in this exquisite representative of Judeo-Arabic 'adab a learned compilation of old and new wisdom and a defense of Judaism in the cross-currents of philosophy and religion in medieval Spain. My book, on the other hand, is addressed quite sincerely to Judd Lewis, and I hope that he will find in it something of value.

The person of Albert Abbadi is a composite of several Jews I have known, but one in particular, a banker who was indeed a Sephardi, though not from Syria. As for his surname, I chose it for (among other reasons) its having belonged to a well known Syrian *ḥazzan* of the last century. Any resemblance of my protagonist to other Abbadis, living or dead, is purely coincidental.

I am grateful to my editor, John Loudon, for having worried with me for many hours about the book's title. The one that we ultimately selected was no one's first choice, but I hope that it in any case will accurately represent the book's subject to a casual browser. I am grateful as well to the friends and colleagues who read drafts of this book and offered suggestions. Their help is deeply appreciated.

—J. K.

Printed in the United States
4455

9 780801 859434